THE WHICH?
HOME SAFETY AND

THE WHICH? GUIDE TO
HOME SAFETY AND
SECURITY

CONSUMERS' ASSOCIATION

Which? Books are commissioned by
Consumers' Association and published by
Which? Ltd, 2 Marylebone Road,
London NW1 4DF

Distributed by The Penguin Group:
Penguin Books Limited, 27 Wrights Lane,
London W8 5TZ

Chapters 1 and 2 by Mike Lawrence
Chapter 3 (sections on car safety and security)
taken from *The Which? Car Owner's Manual*
by Peter Burgess (published September 1994)
The rest of Chapter 3 and Chapter 5 by Sian Morrissey
Chapter 4 by Jonquil Lowe

Typographic design by Paul Saunders
Cover design by Ridgeway Associates
Cover photograph by Britstock - IFA (Bernd Ducke)
Illustrations by Peter Harper

First edition May 1995

British Library Cataloguing in Publication Data
Lawrence, Mike
Which? Guide to Home Safety and Security
I. Title
363.13

ISBN 0 85202 548 3

Typeset by Townsend Typesetter Ltd
Printed and bound by Firmin-Didot (France)
Groupe Herissey
N° d'impression: 30728

With thanks also to the Home Office Crime Prevention Centre,
RoSPA, St John Ambulance; also Graham Kaudeur, Marie Lorimer,
Hugh Morgan and Jennifer Steele

CONTENTS

INTRODUCTION

LIFE is full of unexpected dangers: the statistics prove that. Every year over 4,000 people die and at least three million need medical attention as a result of accidents in the home. House fires kill another 600, while almost 5,000 men, women and children die on our roads annually and many more are injured.

People are not the only casualties either. Nearly a million homes are burgled each year, and fear of burglary is now widespread and increasing. A car is stolen somewhere in the country every minute of the day and night. Even our gardens are under attack, with ornaments, exotic shrubs and expensive powered garden equipment now a favourite target for thieves.

What this book aims to do

Many different organisations and 'watchdogs' work hard to make our lives safer, and the police continue to promise an increasing crackdown on crime. However, there is also much that individuals can do to protect themselves and their families from risk. The majority of accidents in the home and on the road are the result of carelessness and human error, and many of our homes and cars have such poor levels of security that they are an open invitation to criminals. Making our homes safer and our possessions more secure is the simple answer.

The first three sections of the book deal with home safety, home security and safety away from the home. In each section you will find detailed advice on the problems you might face and guidance on how to solve or avoid them. The final sections cover insurance and first aid, the former to ensure that you will be adequately compensated in the event of injury or loss and the latter to help you cope with unexpected medical emergencies correctly.

Throughout the text you will find the names of helpful organisations marked with an asterisk (*); their addresses and telephone numbers can be found in the address section at the back of the book.

A. Keep the shed locked if it contains tools or chemicals

B. Fit self-adhesive film to greenhouse or cold frame panes to prevent them shattering

C. Cover bamboo or other canes with upturned yogurt pots or protective caps to lessen the risk of eye injury

H. Secure climbing frames and swings

I. Don't leave rakes or other garden tools lying around

J. Fill potholes

K. Remove potentially harmful plants if you have young children

L. Fit railings round a patio

M. Avoid leaving hoses or electricity cables uncoiled

N. Take care to avoid trapped fingers when using folding furniture

O. Repair broken steps

P. Attend to cracked, mossy, slippery or uneven paving

Q. Have only a shallow step out of french windows

R. Take care over the positioning of garden ornaments that could topple over

S. Always supervise children in a paddling-pool

T. Don't use paraffin for barbecues or bonfires

U. Don't place a barbecue near something that could catch fire

V. Angle ladders correctly; put them away after use

Prune low overhanging branches
Destroy toadstools
Don't leave weedkiller or other hazardous substances lying around
Never mow the lawn without protective footwear

See pages 37–44 for more about Safety out of doors

CHAPTER 1

HOME SAFETY

The kitchen

One in every six home accidents happens in the kitchen. This is hardly surprising if you consider the potentially dangerous range of equipment and services it contains – hot surfaces, sharp implements, gas and electrical appliances, medicines and household chemicals. The commonest injuries are cuts and puncture wounds, but falls, collisions, burns and poisoning also take their toll, especially on children; almost a third of all kitchen accidents involve the under-14s.

There are numerous causes of kitchen accidents. Simple carelessness is a major factor, but an untidy or badly designed kitchen can raise the danger level, and the presence of small children or elderly people in the family greatly increases the risk of accidents. Here is how to make your kitchen a safer place.

Avoiding cuts and other wounds

Sharp knives and other bladed tools can cause serious injury if they are not handled and stored with care.

● Paradoxically, **the less sharp knives are, the more dangerous they can be** since you will use more pressure to cut things with them and the blade is more likely to slip as a result. Sharpen smooth-bladed knives regularly with a steel or knife sharpener, and buy replacements for blunt knives if they are not suitable for home sharpening.

● **Use knives sensibly.** Never use them to cut things you are holding in your hand; always use a chopping board instead. When carving meat, use a special carving fork to prevent the knife slipping. Take special care when using them to open the packaging on food or household products; a pair of kitchen scissors is often safer. If you must use a knife for this, make sure the tip or cutting edge is pointing away from you so a slip cannot injure you. Never use a knife to prise layers of frozen food apart: the blade is highly likely to slip, and you may break it.

● **Store knives safely**, either in a special cutlery drawer or in a knife block; they will stay sharp for longer if they are not jumbled up together, and you are less likely to cut yourself when selecting the knife you want if they are stored separately. If you have small children in the family, fit a child-resistant safety catch to the drawer or keep the knife block out of reach at the back edge of the worktop. Don't use a magnetic knife rack: the knife blades remain dangerously exposed, and it is easy to knock a knife off the rack accidentally.

● As you work, **always set knives down where you can see them**, and wash them up separately from other kitchen equipment. Don't put them in a sink full of soapy water or you may forget they are there when you plunge in your hands to do the washing up. If you have a dishwasher, always load kitchen knives into the cutlery compartment with the tips pointing downwards, so there is no risk of cutting yourself on an upturned blade when loading other items.

● If you use an **electric carving knife**, unplug it as soon as you have finished using it, then remove the blade for washing. Do not let children use the knife.

● If you use a **blender or food processor**, always unplug it before attempting to clean it or to remove the blades. Never poke a finger or utensil into the machine when it is running, but use the food guide supplied with the processor where applicable.

● Take care when **opening canned foods**; the cut edge of the lid can be very sharp. Cut off the lid completely and push the lid into the can before putting it in the bin, so that you do not risk a cut when binning other rubbish later.

● If you break anything made of **glass**, stop what you are doing and clear up the debris immediately. Keep children and pets away while you do so. Pick up large pieces of glass carefully by hand, then brush or vacuum-clean the area thoroughly to remove small

Safety in the kitchen

A. Keep the fridge door closed
B. Don't keep raw meat on the top shelf; keep raw and cooked foods separate
C. Keep a fire blanket near the cooker
D. Turn saucepan handles to the back of the cooker
E. Don't leave a chip pan to heat up unattended
F. Never put a tea-towel over the hob
G. Don't keep dangerous substances at child height
H. Keep cupboard doors closed; fit child locks if appropriate
I. Keep the oven door closed
J. Clear up toys or broken dishes or glass
K. Keep pets away from food preparation areas
L. Don't leave an iron unattended, especially if it is hot
M. Keep work surfaces clean and floors dry
N. Don't leave knives lying around
O. Never lift a hot pan or dish and carry a child at the same time
P. Avoid dangling flexes: use short curly flex where appropriate

slivers that are often almost invisible to the naked eye. Wrap the debris in newspaper or kitchen roll, bag it up and put it in the dustbin.

Avoiding burns and scalds

The main causes of burns are contact with a hot hob or the oven or with hot cooking utensils. Small children are especially at risk from contact with glass doors on ovens and washer-driers, and also from playing with matches if these are left within reach. Scalding by hot liquids is commonly the result of accidental spillage; a cup of tea or coffee can be hot enough to scald 15 minutes after being made. Treatment for severe burns and scalds can be long and painful. See page 191 for first aid treatment.

- **Turn off gas burners and electric hob elements** when you have finished with them. Remember that electric elements remain hot enough to burn you – or anything combustible that may inadvertently be placed over them, such as a tea-towel – for some time after they have been switched off. Allow hobs and ovens to cool down before cleaning them.
- Always use **oven gloves** or a thick dry cloth to remove hot dishes from ovens. Otherwise, you not only risk burning your hands but you may also drop the dish, scalding yourself and probably damaging the kitchen floor into the bargain.
- **Keep small children away** from the hob and oven – especially its glass door, unless you have a cool-touch type – when you are cooking. Fit an oven door cover to protect children when the oven is in use. For extra safety, use only rear burners or elements or turn the handles of pans on front burners away from the front of the cooker so that they are out of reach and cannot be toppled on to a toddler. Fit a hob guard if you wish, but make sure it does not impede the cook's safe access to the burners or controls.
- Take care when moving **saucepans** from hob to sink to drain off the hot water.
- Use a short or coiled flex for your **electric kettle** (or buy a cordless kettle) so the flex cannot hang over the edge of the worktop and be pulled by a child; such action could cause severe

scalding. For extra safety, keep the kettle at the back of the worktop and always empty a boiled kettle after use.

● Never leave an **electric iron** unattended when it is plugged in if you have small children. A child could pull it off the ironing board by its flex, burning or otherwise injuring himself or herself and possibly damaging furnishings or floorcoverings too.

● Over a third of burns and scalds happen to the **under-fives**. Don't hold a child when having a hot drink, or leave hot drinks unattended within children's reach.

Avoiding falls and collisions

There are three common causes of falls in the kitchen. A major risk is using something inappropriate to gain access to a high shelf. You can also trip on a mat or other object on the floor, or slip and lose your footing because the floor is wet after cleaning or a spillage. Collisions with open cupboard or appliance doors or with other members of the family – especially small children and pets – can also result in injury, especially if you are carrying something at the time and drop it as a result.

● **Use proper kitchen steps** or a hop-up rather than a chair to reach high shelves. Make sure you have a good grip on heavy objects before lifting them down, and that you have somewhere to put them down safely before stepping down yourself.

● Do not put **babies** on kitchen tables or worktops, and discourage **toddlers** from trying to climb on to them. A fall can happen in a split second.

● If you have a washable **floor** surface, mop it dry after washing it and wipe up liquid spillages thoroughly as soon as they occur. Never use polish on a smooth kitchen floor surface. If you must have mats in the room, fit slip-resistant strips to their undersides.

● Get in the habit of closing **doors and drawers** every time you use them, so that no one can bump into them.

● Keep the **floor clear of clutter** at all times. If you have to have small children in the room with you, ideally confine them to a playpen. Have a 'Walk, don't run' rule for older children, especially if the room contains an external door to the side or rear of the house which they use for access.

Avoiding poisoning

The under-fives are most at risk of poisoning in the kitchen; over 85 per cent of incidents involve this age-group. Most kitchens contain a large assortment of household products, many of which are highly unpleasant or even toxic if ingested by the curious but unwitting toddler. Dishwasher liquid and powder, for instance, are very corrosive. Many people also keep medicines in the kitchen, and, despite the introduction of child-resistant closures for most medicinal products, accidents still happen. A completely unrelated danger that can affect all ages equally is carbon monoxide poisoning, caused by faulty fuel-burning appliances or inadequate room ventilation.

- Store **all household chemicals and medicines** out of reach and out of sight of small children, preferably in a lockable cupboard. Buy potentially dangerous household products such as bleach and white spirit in child-resistant containers wherever possible. Never decant chemicals into other containers. Dispose of unwanted medicines by returning them to a pharmacy; do not flush them down the WC or pour them down the sink. See pages 63–5 for more information.
- Have **fuel-burning appliances**, such as central-heating boilers and water heaters that are located in the kitchen, serviced regularly, and get expert advice from your fuel supplier if you are unsure whether the room has adequate ventilation. If you ever experience drowsiness in the room when an appliance is operating, turn it off and get expert advice immediately. You can fit a carbon monoxide detector in the room as an additional safeguard if you wish, although one should not be necessary if the appliance is in good working order and the ventilation is adequate.

Avoiding a fire

More fires are started in the kitchen than in any other room in the house. A moment's carelessness can easily result in a small fire which may, given the right conditions, soon become uncontrollable.

- If you use a **chip pan** or a **wok**, take care not to let it get too hot and never leave it unattended. Buy a thermostatically controlled chip fryer if you prefer fried to baked chips.

- Keep **combustible materials** – tea-towels, kitchen roll and so on – well away from the hob area. Do not drape tea-towels over a plate rack above the hob in case they fall on to a hot burner or element.
- Never decorate a kitchen ceiling with **polystyrene tiles**. A flash of flame from the hob could ignite the tiles, spreading the fire across the room in seconds.
- Keep a **fire blanket** in a wall-mounted holder within easy reach of the hob in case of accidents. It is best not to fit a smoke alarm in a kitchen, since cooking can cause regular nuisance alarms. See pages 49–52 for more information about safety from fire.

Avoiding other accidents

There are plenty of other ways of injuring yourself in a typical kitchen. You can splash things in your eyes, choke on your food, get stung by an insect, electrocute yourself, blow yourself up or fall over the family dog.

- Keep an **eyebath** in the kitchen so that you can quickly wash out your eyes if you splash something into them. A bottle of eyewash is useful but not essential; clean tap-water is the best instant remedy.
- Keep a fly-swatter or aerosol insect killer in the kitchen so you can deal with **flies and wasps**, but don't spray near the hob. Usher bees out of an open window.
- Make sure that all **electrical appliances are in good working order**, that flexes are undamaged and that the plug fuse is of the correct rating for the appliance. The rule of thumb is that anything that heats (more than 690 watts) needs a 13-amp fuse; other appliances using up to 690 watts need a 3-amp fuse. Put appliances away when you have finished using them. Take care not to trail flexes across hot hobs. Don't use portable appliances next to the sink or plug them in with wet hands. Avoid using adaptors; have extra sockets installed if you need them. Take care not to overload the power circuit by plugging in too many high-wattage appliances – those with heating elements – at the same time.
- If a **gas** burner, grill or oven does not ignite quickly, turn the gas supply off, open a window and fan away the fumes before trying again.

● Keep family **pets** out of the kitchen when you are working in the room unless there is space for a bed well out of the way. Teach cats firmly not to go on the worktops, for obvious food hygiene reasons.

You will find more information on safety with gas, electricity and electrical appliances on page 55, and on safety with pets on page 77.

Common-sense precautions

Because so many accidents in the home are caused by human error, a little care and common sense are often all that is needed to prevent them. The special dangers the kitchen holds mean that extra thought and extra care are essential at all times. Whatever you are doing, think about potential dangers both to yourself and to other members of the family, concentrate on what you are doing and try to keep distractions to a minimum. Your kitchen will be a far safer place as a result. Lastly, if you have young children, put them in a playpen or use a child safety barrier to keep them out of the kitchen altogether while you work. They are twice as likely as you to have an accident there.

Food safety

Food poisoning is an increasingly common problem in the home, for reasons which may reflect changes in methods of food production and preparation, or in our tastes and eating habits. Official statistics do not give a complete picture because many cases are not reported to doctors; thankfully, the illness that food poisoning causes is usually relatively mild and short-lived, and most people prefer to treat themselves as a result. However, certain bacteria and the toxins they produce can cause severe illness and occasionally death. It is therefore vital to know what you can do in your home to minimise the risk of an outbreak.

Shopping wisely

Food shops have a legal requirement under the Food Safety Act 1990 to sell only food that is safe to eat, and local authority environmental health officers have a duty to inspect shops regularly and to prosecute offenders. Despite this, recent surveys have found alarmingly poor standards of food hygiene, especially in shops such as butchers and delicatessens where staff are likely to handle unwrapped food. Supermarkets generally perform better, although counters selling unwrapped food can still pose problems.

Shop hygiene

When shopping for food, look for the following good hygiene practices, and beware premises that fail on any count:

- Staff handling food should wear **clean protective clothing**, have their hair covered and wash their hands between handling raw and cooked foods.
- Staff should use **separate tongs, film-wrap or gloves** to handle raw and cooked foods (and gloves when handling money).
- **Cooked and raw meats** should be stored separately.
- **Surfaces** that food could come into contact with should be cleaned regularly with a bactericide or a detergent and a clean disposable cloth.

Best-before dates

Always check the 'best-before' or 'use-by' dates on packaged food. If individual packs of a particular product are on sale with different dates, pick the latest available. Get fresh, chilled or frozen food home as quickly as possible; if it gets warm, any bacteria present will start to grow more quickly than if the food is kept well chilled. It is a good idea to use an insulated cool bag if you take longer than about an hour to get your food home.

Storing food correctly

The biggest danger is from cross-contamination; raw and cooked food must be stored separately in your fridge, ideally with raw food at the bottom where it cannot drip on to cooked food. Raw food is more likely to contain bacteria than cooked.

- To limit the growth of bacteria in stored food, your **fridge** should operate at a **temperature of 5°C or less**. Few fridges have a thermometer, so buy one, hang it in your fridge and check the temperature regularly, altering the thermostat setting as necessary. Try to avoid overloading the fridge, and always check that the door is firmly closed after use. Replace the door seals if they show signs of perishing or physical damage.

● It is a good idea to check your **freezer temperature** regularly too (you can buy combined fridge/freezer thermometers) to ensure that the temperature is as close as possible to the ideal level of −18°C.

● **Keep the fridge clean**, and defrost it regularly if it's got a frozen food compartment.

● Follow the **storage instructions** on the food packaging to the letter. Discard unused food stored past its best-before or use-by date. For both shop- and home-frozen food, check the storage times recommended for different food types by the freezer manufacturer, and date the packaging or container with a use-by label before storing it.

● If you intend to store freshly cooked food or leftovers, avoid handling them unnecessarily. Cover them, cool them quickly and put them in the fridge. Use them within two days.

Handling food safely

Bacteria can get into uncontaminated food because of poor kitchen hygiene practices. Follow these guidelines to ensure that your kitchen is a safe place to prepare and handle food:

● **Wash your hands** with soap and hot water before handling food, and always after using the WC.

● **Keep work surfaces and utensils clean**. Wash anything you drop on the floor before re-using it.

● **Use separate chopping boards and knives** for raw meat, cooked meat and vegetables. Smooth waterproof plastic boards are more hygienic than wooden ones; scrub all boards with detergent and hot water after use so that their surfaces cannot harbour bacteria.

● **Change washing-up cloths and tea-towels** every day, and immerse washing-up brushes in diluted bleach regularly.

● Keep **pets** off work surfaces at all times, and don't touch them during food handling or preparation.

Cooking food properly

Thorough cooking kills the bacteria that cause food poisoning. To ensure this, every part of the dish should reach a temperature of at least 70°C (160°F) – too hot to eat immediately. If you use a conventional oven, pre-heat it to the required temperature, put the food on a pre-heated baking tray and use the centre shelf (unless the cooking instructions say otherwise) to make the food heat up more quickly. Remember that the more dishes are put in the oven, the longer the cooking time is likely to be. If you use a microwave oven, follow the oven manufacturer's and food packaging instructions carefully, including any requirement for a standing time after cooking, and check before serving that the food is heated evenly throughout the dish. New ovens and current food packaging should have labels that make it easier to match these two separate sets of instructions.

Avoid storing cooked food in the fridge for more than two days. If you have to prepare a dish for consumption at a much later date, freeze it as soon as you have prepared it and allowed it to cool. Never reheat chilled dishes more than once.

Washing up

If you wash up by hand, use detergent and the hottest water you can stand, and rinse dishes and utensils under the hot tap after washing them. If possible, allow them to drip-dry on a clean rack, or use a clean tea-towel every time; used towels can harbour bacteria.

A dishwasher is more hygienic than hand-washing, because of the high temperature the water reaches. Clean the filters regularly, and wipe the door seals and edges regularly to prevent a build-up of food residues.

Natural food toxins

Some foods contain toxic chemicals that can cause illness and occasionally death. In plant foods they may be made naturally; in other foods they may be the result of action by bacteria, fungi or algae. Here is how to guard against some of their effects:

- **Potatoes**: store them in a cool dark place, and cut away any sprouts or green parts before cooking.
- **Hard foods** such as cabbage, carrots, broccoli, onions, apples, pears and Cheddar cheese: cut away mouldy, bruised or damaged parts plus some of the surrounding sound parts.
- **Soft foods** such as tomatoes, cucumbers, bananas, spinach, bread, yogurt and other dairy products: discard completely if mouldy.
- **Nuts**: throw away any that smell or taste musty.
- **Shellfish**: avoid buying local produce in coastal areas where warning notices about toxic algal blooms are displayed. The period from April to September is the time of greatest risk.
- **Imported fish** such as red snapper, sea bream and barracuda: choose small fish if possible, and do not eat the guts or roe of the fish.

Food by mail order

Foods such as clotted cream, smoked salmon and other cooked or smoked meat, poultry and game are widely available from mail-order suppliers. Since they are exempt from the storage temperature requirements of shop-bought products, they may reach relatively high temperatures on their travels through the post, and this can cause any bacteria in the food to multiply. To minimise the risk when ordering such food, follow these guidelines:

- Use companies that can **guarantee delivery within 24 hours** of despatch, or which guarantee chilled delivery or use insulated packaging and coolants.
- Put the food in the fridge as soon as it arrives, and **eat it within two days** (or by the use-by date if it was chilled when delivered).
- If **sending the food as a gift**, find out when delivery is likely and advise the recipient (you do not have to say what you are sending).
- If the **inner packaging** is swollen or damaged, or you are unsure about the smell or appearance of the food, don't eat it and notify the supplier immediately.

Living areas

Accidents in living areas of the house – the living-room, dining-room and bedrooms – account for over 30 per cent of the total, more than

Safety in the living-room

A. Don't leave bags or other valuables in view from outside the house
B. Don't have flexes trailing across floors or under carpets
C. Don't leave aerosols and other chemicals near to a source of heat
D. Don't dry clothes next to the fire
E. Avoid rucked up rugs and carpets
F. Clear up toys and other objects that could be tripped over
G. Don't leave matches or cigarettes lying around, especially lit ones
H. Get rid of old foam-filled furniture, and keep climbable furniture away from windows
I. Keep low-level windows locked
J. Keep a key to open double glazing in an accessible place in case of fire
K. Don't overload electric sockets, and avoid using adaptors
L. Fit a guard in front of open fires

in any other part of the home. The nature of the furnishings and fittings in these rooms poses different dangers to those faced in the kitchen; falls and collisions are the commonest cause of injury in living areas, but a wide range of other dangers may also be present, ranging from obvious candidates, such as open fires, to less expected hazards, such as low-level glazing. Every home and family will face different risks, according to the family make-up and lifestyle; read through the following sections so that you can identify and be aware of problems that affect your own circumstances.

Avoiding falls and collisions

Elderly people are especially at risk if living alone, since they may be unable to get up after a fall and are therefore in danger not only from the effects of any injury they may have sustained but also from hypothermia and dehydration as a result of their immobility.

- **Keep the floors** of living-rooms and bedrooms **clear of obstacles**, especially along traffic routes. This is particularly important in bedrooms, where an obstacle clearly visible in daylight – even something as seemingly innocuous as the trailing end of a quilt or bedcover – can become a major trip hazard in the dark. Be ruthless about **children's toys** left on the floor; they can be more dangerous to an adult than to a child, as anyone who has stepped on a small wheeled toy in a polished parquet hallway will testify. Teach your children at the earliest possible age to put their toys away when they have finished playing with them, and don't let temper tantrums deter you from clearing the decks at regular intervals.
- Low tables and other **low-level furniture** in living-rooms are a trip hazard for adults. They are also a source of secondary danger for small children, who can easily reach potentially dangerous things such as hot or alcoholic drinks, cigarettes, matches and lighters. If you have children, keep all such furniture away from open or openable windows to prevent children from climbing up to them, and avoid having glass-topped tables or display cabinets with glass doors unless the glass is laminated or toughened. Don't place babies on low tables or other furniture from which they can easily fall if left unsupervised.

- Make sure that **carpets** are securely fitted, especially in door openings. Replace worn areas of carpets (or cover the area with a securely fixed patch as a temporary measure). Avoid using loose rugs altogether in traffic areas, especially on top of smooth fitted floorcoverings, and secure rugs used elsewhere with slip-resistant tape.

- Do not let **flexes to electrical appliances** trail across any likely traffic routes. Tuck them behind furniture wherever possible and protect them with special rubber cover strips otherwise; do not thread them underneath the carpet. Avoid using table lamps if you have toddlers in the family; a yank on the lamp flex could pull the lamp over and injure the child.

- Make sure you can turn on at least one light in the room from a **switch by the door**, so you do not have to blunder about in the dark at night.

- If you have **sliding patio doors** or internal glazed doors, stick some form of visual warning to the glass to lessen the risk of someone trying to walk through a closed door. You can obtain peelable semi-transparent strips from door retailers, or use any form of self-adhesive sticker. Cartoon characters and the like can help catch children's attention if stuck on at a low level. See also Avoiding accidents with glass, overleaf.

- Check that elderly people have **well-fitting footwear** in good condition. Loose and badly worn shoes and slippers cause many falls in this age-group.

Avoiding accidents with furniture

- Fix tall, slim **bookcases and display cabinets** to the wall at the top rear edge to prevent them from toppling over if unevenly loaded or climbed by a child. Use simple angle brackets or proprietary fixing devices.

- Secure the shelves of **adjustable track shelving systems** to their brackets so that a collision does not disturb the shelf or its contents. Round off shelf corners if they are exposed.

- Do not place **furniture with castors** close to low-level glazing. An adult sitting down heavily or a child leaping aboard could cause the chair to move suddenly and break the window.

- Take care with **furniture that folds away** for storage. It is easy to trap fingers in the mechanism or between the folding parts.

● Children and **rocking-chairs** do not mix. The design of the chairs not only encourages boisterous but potentially dangerous horseplay, but a rocking-chair can trap small fingers between the rocker and the floor or between a frame-mounted chair and its base.

Avoiding accidents with glass

Living-rooms often have large areas of glazing, especially in doors leading to the garden, and may also contain furniture with glass shelves, glazed doors and glass table-tops, as well as wine glasses and glass ornaments.

As mentioned on page 25, patio doors pose a hazard to anyone unaware that the door is closed; visible warning strips on the glass can help to reduce this risk, and you can stick special shatter-resistant window film to the glass as an extra security precaution if the existing glass is not safety glass. If you are fitting such doors or installing any new low-level glazing, use only toughened or laminated glass. It is wise to specify toughened glass for the tops, shelves and doors of any furniture, too, especially if you have children or elderly people in the family.

Avoiding accidents with fire

The fire risk in your living areas depends on two main factors: whether you have any form of radiant heating equipment and whether anyone in the family is a smoker. See also the section on fire on page 49 for more information.

● If you use an **open fire**, always fit a fire-guard to prevent hot sparks from reaching combustible materials near the fireplace. Use a guard with fuel-effect gas fires, too, to stop clothing catching fire if someone stands too close to the fireplace. Guards should not be free-standing: devise some form of simple hook or child-resistant catch to keep them securely in position. Get your chimney swept regularly if you have an open fire.

● Never remove the protective guard on an **electric radiant heater**.

● **Never dry clothes** on airers standing close to any fire, as items could fall off or be dislodged accidentally and might fall into the flames or touch the heating element. Never dry or air clothes over a convector heater: blocking the air vents could cause the elements to overheat and set fire to the clothes.

- If anyone in the family **smokes**, ensure that you have an adequate supply of ashtrays. Choose types without side rests, from which an unattended cigarette could fall and ignite furniture or floorcoverings. Check that cigarettes are completely extinguished before emptying ashtrays into waste-paper baskets or rubbish bins. Never smoke in bed; fit a linked smoke detector in the bedroom of elderly smokers.
- If you have small children in the family, keep **smokers' materials** totally out of their reach at all times.

Avoiding accidents with electricity

So long as electrical appliances in living areas are in good working order, there should be no danger arising from using them.

- Make sure that **flexes** are out of the way of traffic areas. Check that the correct fuse is fitted to match the appliance wattage (see page 59 for more details) and that plugs and sockets are undamaged. Avoid the use of adaptors so that you do not overload sockets physically or electrically; buy special multi-way adaptors to cope with the demands of home-entertainment equipment.
- If you have small children in the family, fit snap-on or plug-in **socket guards** to all unused sockets to prevent small fingers or other unauthorised objects being poked into the holes. Make sure that all appliances in use are fitted with plugs having sleeved live and neutral pins. Avoid the use of lamps on low tables, and position home-entertainment equipment out of reach or in cabinets with child-resistant catches.
- Have **electric blankets** serviced every three or four years by the manufacturer. If yours is found to be faulty, it is better (and often little more expensive) to replace it with a new blanket than to have it repaired.
- If you use a **sun-bed or sun-lamp**, always wear eye protection and take care not to exceed the manufacturer's recommended exposure times. If you have ever fallen asleep on a sun-bed, set an

alarm clock or kitchen timer to wake you so you cannot be accidentally burned in future.

Avoiding problems with ventilation

An unseen danger in rooms containing fuel-burning appliances is a build-up of poisonous carbon monoxide (CO) as a result of poor appliance maintenance or inadequate ventilation.

- Have **appliances serviced** every year by a qualified engineer.
- Get **chimneys** swept regularly and check that flue outlet grilles are unobstructed.
- Fit a **CO detector** in rooms containing fuel-burning appliances. An inexpensive type giving a visual warning of a CO build-up is adequate in living-rooms, but one with an audible alarm (rather more expensive) is essential in bedrooms.

The bathroom

The bathroom is a comparatively low-risk zone as far as personal accident and injury are concerned, probably because we spend relatively little time in there compared with other areas of the house. Falls, chiefly in the bath or shower, account for almost half the accident statistics here; collisions, cuts (mainly from shaving), problems with foreign bodies, such as cotton wool buds, and scalding injuries make up the bulk of the rest, with a solitary bathroom explosion also recorded in the latest available figures.

Avoiding falls and collisions

Wet surfaces are the main cause of falls, and of the subsequent injuries sustained by striking a surface or an item of bathroom equipment. The very young and very old are most at risk. The consequences of a fall are often exacerbated by the victim being naked or partly clothed and bare-footed.

- Use **non-slip mats** in the bath and in shower cubicles, especially for children and the elderly. Avoid the use of bath oils, especially in soft-water areas; if you must have a 'fragrant' bath, bath salts do not make the bath as dangerously slippery.

Safety in the bathroom

A. Make sure the mirror is hung securely

B. Keep the medicine cabinet out of reach of children and securely locked

C. Never leave a small child unattended in the bath

D. Use a non-slip mat in the bath and shower to help prevent falls

E. Avoid pools of water on smooth floorcoverings

F. Don't leave bleach or other hazardous substances lying around, especially with the lid off

G. Check that exposed metalwork is properly earthed

H. Never use any electrical appliances in the bathroom with the help of an extension cable; socket outlets are not allowed, except for electric shavers

---

● Bathe **young children** one at a time if possible, and never leave a small child alone in the bath. Drowning can occur within seconds, and can happen in as little as 75mm (3in) of water.

● If there are elderly or disabled people in the household, provide plenty of **hand grips**, both for general support and to assist them in using the bath, shower or WC. See page 75 for more details.

● If you have a **smooth floorcovering** in the bathroom, use a bathmat to absorb splashes and drips so that the floor does not become unnecessarily slippery, and dry the floor after each use of the bath or shower. Lift the bathmat off the floor when you have finished using it.

● If you are **replacing the bathroom floorcovering**, choose a non-slip type – textured vinyl, rubber or water-resistant carpet are all more slip-resistant than smooth tiles or vinyl sheeting.

● Keep the bathroom floor clear of **clutter** – clothes, towels, toys and so on.

Avoiding cuts

Razor blades and broken glass are the main causes of bathroom accidents.

● Use **razors** with captive strip blades in preference to those with replaceable double-edged blades. Dispose of used razors and blades safely, and keep spare razors and blades well out of the reach of children. Never remove a blade from the razor for tasks such as shaving corns, but use proper pedicure equipment. For complete safety, use a mains- or battery-powered electric razor instead.

● Keep **scissors**, nail clippers and other bladed tools out of reach of young children.

● Avoid the use of **glass and china containers** in the bathroom; dropping one and breaking it will scatter sharp pieces of glass or ceramic glaze around the room. Most toiletries and bathroom cleaners are readily available in safe plastic bottles and jars. If you use a container to store toothbrushes, choose a plastic one rather than using a glass or a china mug.

● Make sure that shower screens, glass splashbacks and shelves are of **safety glass** so they will not shatter into sharp shards if you fall against them. Rigid plastic sheeting is a safe alternative for bath and shower screens. Small wall-mounted mirrors are generally perfectly safe, but safety glass is a must for full-length mirrors.

● Use light fittings that enclose the bulb completely. You can have a pendant light or a ceiling-mounted batten lampholder in a bathroom as long as it is fitted with a special protective skirt to prevent access to live parts, but there is always a risk of the bulb being broken accidentally – by a carelessly wielded towel, for example, or as a result of splashed water cracking the hot glass.

Avoiding scalding

The under-fives are especially at risk from scalding in the bathroom. A shower without a thermostatic control can cause unexpected scalding if water is drawn off elsewhere in the house while it is in use.

- Always test the **temperature of bathwater** before bathing small children.
- Run **cold water into the bath first**, then add hot water as required. Remember that your hand can usually stand hotter water than the rest of your body.
- Fit a **thermostatic shower mixer** or mains-fed shower unit.
- Keep the **domestic hot-water temperature** at a maximum of 54°C (130°F) for absolute safety.

Avoiding poisoning

Apart from the kitchen, more poisoning incidents occur in the bathroom than anywhere else in the house. The under-fives are by far the commonest victims.

- Keep all **medicines, toiletries and bathroom cleaning chemicals** out of sight and out of reach of children. Medicines should ideally be kept in a lockable cupboard. Chemicals should be in containers with child-resistant closures. Do not leave bleach to stand in the WC bowl; it could badly injure an inquisitive child and can give an unpleasant surprise to a later user of the WC who may be unaware of its presence.
- If the room contains a **gas-powered water or space heater**, have it serviced regularly to ensure that it burns efficiently and is properly ventilated so that it cannot create a potentially dangerous build-up of carbon monoxide in the room.

Avoiding electric shock

Contrary to popular belief, the bathroom is very safe electrically; the latest statistics on home accidents record no reported cases of electric shock injuries there. Modern wiring regulations go a long way towards ensuring that the bathroom is a safe zone by banning socket outlets (except shaver supply units) and any wall switches within

31

reach of a bath or shower, and unless you are stupid enough to use an electrical appliance supplied by an extension lead from another room in the bathroom you should be safe.

- Unless you are an experienced d-i-y electrician with an up-to-date knowledge of the wiring regulations, have any **electrical work** in the bathroom carried out by a qualified electrician.
- Check that all **exposed metalwork** in the bathroom – plumbing pipes, towel rails, the bath if it is metal – is cross-bonded to earth by special green and yellow earth cables and earth clamps. Earlier d-i-y plumbing or wiring work in the room may not have included this vital safety feature. If there is no cross-bonding visible, call in an electrician to install it immediately (and get him to check the rest of the earthing system while he is doing so).
- For total safety, have any **mains-voltage equipment** in the bathroom protected by a residual current device (RCD), or choose low-voltage equipment such as light fittings, extractor fans and shower pumps, and ensure that all light bulbs are completely enclosed.

The stairs

Stairs are dangerous. Falls on an inside staircase are responsible for over 500 deaths and roughly a quarter of a million injuries in the home each year. The elderly are by far the likeliest age-group to die as a result of such a fall: about 70 per cent of those deaths were of people over 65. A third of the injuries involve children under the age of 14. We should clearly be building more bungalows.

A. Don't allow small children to play on the stairs
B. Fit child safety barriers at the top and bottom of the stairs
C. Fit two-way light switches at the top and bottom of the stairs, and ensure that stairwell lighting illuminates treads evenly
D. Take care on very steep, narrow stairs
E. Fit a smoke detector in the hall ceiling above the foot of the stairs, ideally linked to a second one on the landing
F. Check that rails and balusters are secure and undamaged
G. Don't leave items such as laundry, shoes and toys on the stairs
H. Replace worn stair carpet, and avoid loose rugs on or near stairs
I. Fit a handrail if none exists – this will help particularly if the stairs are steep or narrow

Safety on the stairs

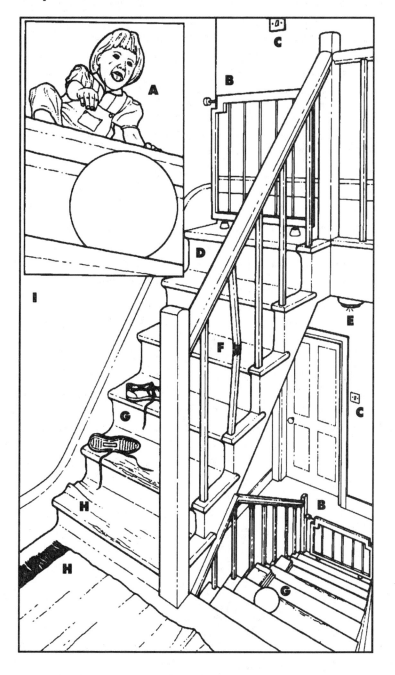

The current Building Regulations contain precise requirements for the steepness of domestic staircases, the number of treads per flight, the layout of landings and, most importantly, the provision of handrails and guarding both on landings and alongside the flight itself where necessary. Unfortunately, there are several million homes in the country that were built before the introduction of these standards, and many of them still have staircases that are too steep, too long and with inadequate or dangerous handrails and guarding.

Avoiding falls and collisions

Tripping is the biggest danger on the staircase. The cause may be loose or worn floorcoverings on or near the flight, obstacles left on the treads, a collision with someone else (or a pet) using the flight, badly fitting footwear, poor lighting, sudden dizziness due to illness or medication, children at play or simple carelessness. Adequate handrails and guarding may help to stop a trip turning into a fall, but only continuous care on the stairs can prevent accidents.

- Keep the stair treads clear of **obstacles** at all times. It may be tempting to save your legs by placing things on one or more of the treads ready to be carried upstairs later, but they could literally be the cause of your downfall.
- Do not allow your **children** to play on the stairs. Not only is there the very real risk of them falling and sustaining a serious injury, but the presence of **toys** on the flight could cause an accident to someone else. Make it a house rule that there is to be *no* running on the stairs under any circumstances.
- If you have babies or toddlers in the family, fit a **safety gate or barrier** at the top and/or the bottom of the stairs, following the manufacturer's instructions. Choose one made to British Standard BS4125, and check its features to ensure that it is convenient for adults to open or remove as necessary; if it is awkward to negotiate, there is a chance that it will not be used all the time, and crawlers need only one chance to escape confinement. Some safety barriers come with additional fittings that enable them to be used in doorways elsewhere around the house – to keep a child in a particular room or out of the kitchen, for example.
- Keep **pets** off the stairs. They can get under your feet and may

rush past you as you ascend or descend, causing you to lose your balance or footing. In any case, it is unhygienic to allow them into bedrooms (and especially on the beds); dogs soon learn where they are not permitted, and even a cat can be trained with persistence.

- Make sure that the **stair treads** themselves are not a hazard. If the flight is carpeted, make sure that a fitted carpet is held taut and securely by gripper strips, that a runner is held tightly by stair rods, and that the fixings holding the latter in place are sound. Re-fix carpet that works loose, and replace any badly worn areas of carpet.

- If you have an **open-plan staircase**, polished wooden treads may look attractive but they can be a danger, especially to the young, the old and anyone using the flight in socks or stockinged feet. If you want to retain the look of such a flight, either stick two parallel strips of non-slip tape to each tread near the nosing or tack pieces of carpet to the tread surfaces.

- Do not place **loose rugs** close to the top of the flight, especially if you have a smooth floorcovering on the landing. Avoid rugs in the hall, too, if possible; fit them with non-slip underlay if you must have them there as part of your decor.

- Be aware of the dangers of wearing **long, loose clothing and poorly fitting footwear**, both of which can contribute to falls on stairs. Backless slippers and long nightdresses and dressing-gowns are a particular hazard both for elderly and very young people.

- If you are carrying out any **d-i-y activity** in the stairwell, always remember how dangerous an environment it can be and watch where you step as you work. If you are using access equipment, position it carefully and if possible secure or restrain it so that it cannot move or be dislodged as you use it. For example, nail battens to the treads to prevent the foot of a ladder section from slipping, and tie planks or trestles to their supports. The best access equipment for time-consuming jobs such as decorating a stairwell is a slot-together platform tower, but a combination stepladder is an acceptable alternative for smaller jobs. See also page 44.

- Above all, **take great care** whenever you use the stairs, especially if you are descending them or carrying something – a baby, a tray, a pile of clothes or an armful of toys. Look where you are going, and use the handrail if you have a free hand. If your flight has tapered treads, try to use the widest part of each tread.

Improving safety on the stairs

Apart from taking these common-sense precautions, there are several other steps you can take to make sure your stairs are safe to use.

- Make sure that the **stairwell is brightly lit**, with light directed from above so that it throws the risers into shadow and highlights clearly the positions of the treads. A single pendant light on the landing ceiling is better than nothing, but a more effective solution is to install an evenly spaced series of downlighters there so that each tread is lit directly from above. This arrangement also has an additional safety advantage: the flight will not be plunged into darkness if a light bulb fails, as it would be if you relied on a single pendant fitting. If you prefer to use spotlights rather than down-lighters, position them carefully to avoid glare.

- Provide **full two-way switching** of the stairwell lighting, so you can turn the lights on and off from both hall and landing and avoid having to negotiate the flight in the dark. It is not difficult to convert your existing switch arrangement to two-way operation. All you have to do is install a two-way two-gang switch at each level, wire each light into one gang of the switch nearest to it and then link the individual gangs of the two switches with special three-core-and-earth cable. If you do not feel confident of your electrical knowledge or your ability to do the conversion safely, call in a qualified electrician to carry it out for you.

- If you dislike wasting electricity and have a family that never switches lights off, **install a time delay switch** to control the stairwell lighting. This will turn the lights off automatically at a pre-set time after they have been turned on; you can set this at anything from two to fifteen minutes. Alternatively, consider the use of extra-low-voltage (ELV) lighting run from a transformer, and leave the lights on continuously; switching them on and off actually shortens the lamp life dramatically.

- If you have children or regular overnight guests, it is a good idea to provide some **low-level lighting on the landing** during the night to light the way to the bathroom. You can fit a dimmer switch to control the landing light, but if you have a socket outlet on the landing an alternative is to use a glow-plug. This looks like an ordinary plug but contains a small lamp so it glows when plugged in, and is designed for use as a bedroom night-light for children.

- Check that **stair handrails and balustrades** are securely fixed, and make immediate repairs to any loose fixings or damaged components. Fit a handrail at each side of the flight if it will be used by an elderly person, and add another rail at a lower level – about 600mm (2ft) above the flight – for children to use. You can remove it when they can reach the main handrail.
- Make sure that the design of the stair balustrade cannot assist children to climb it. Check that the **balusters** are no more than 100mm (4in) apart, and add vertical infill components if they are. If stair treads are open, fit tie rods between the treads to reduce the gap width.

Out of doors

The garden is as big a danger area as any part of the house; about a sixth of all accidents occur there, and there are plenty of hazards to contend with – some obvious, others unexpected. Falls and collisions with things make up the bulk of the accident statistics, but injuries sustained when using gardening and d-i-y tools, especially powered ones, figure prominently too, even though many new tools have improved safety features. Other dangers include folding garden furniture, animal and insect bites, foreign bodies (especially in the eyes), drowning accidents in garden ponds or in paddling- and swimming-pools, poisoning from garden chemicals, and, last but by no means least, sunburn or over-exertion. Even playing in the garden can be dangerous, especially for children. Thankfully, shocks and electrocutions are now comparatively rare; the message about using RCDs as protective devices when working with mains-powered equipment out of doors has obviously been heard. However, there is much else to look out for.

Avoiding falls

The danger of a fall begins at the door threshold, and is increased if your garden has features such as a raised patio or balcony, steps between levels and steep slopes. Rather surprisingly, more people fall from ladders and steps indoors than they do outside the home;

perhaps they are more aware of the dangers and so take extra care. See D-i-y safety on page 44 for more details.

● If you have to **step down** more than about 230mm (9in) when leaving your front or back door, add an intermediate step measuring at least 300mm (12in) from front to back and extending the full width of the threshold. Make sure the tread slopes slightly so that water drains freely off it in wet weather and cannot freeze to ice in winter.

● Make sure that **raised patios and balconies** have railings or other guarding at least 900mm (3ft) high for safety, and that the design of the guarding does not encourage children to climb it. Check regularly that railings are securely fixed and free from rust, that any wood used is sound and unaffected by rot, and that masonry is in good condition; frost can weaken the horizontal bond between courses, allowing sections to collapse if someone falls heavily against them.

● Any **steps** built in the garden should have treads measuring at least 300mm (12in) from front to back and a minimum of 600mm (2ft) wide. The tread width should be more than doubled to 1.5m (5ft) if people will need to pass each other on the flight of steps. Flights of more than ten treads should have an intermediate landing.

● Provide **strong handrails** or build walls at both sides of flights of steps containing more than three or four steps, especially free-standing ones.

● Keep all **hard surfaces** – patios, paths, drives and steps – in good condition. Pot-holes, paving slabs that have cracked or subsided and loose step treads can all be trip hazards, and surfaces that have become covered with moss or algal growth can be very slippery in wet weather.

● Try to keep **obstacles** in the garden to a minimum so that you cannot trip over them. Coil up garden hoses and electrical extension leads as soon as you have finished using them, and put wheelbarrows, watering-cans and gardening tools – especially bladed ones – away safely at the end of the day. If you use a rake of any sort, get in the habit of leaving it flat on the ground with the tines facing down; otherwise, you could impale a foot on a wire lawn rake, and a garden rake could spring to the vertical and strike you if you trod on the blade.

● Never work in the garden in **bare feet**. Shoes or boots will give you a safe grip, and will also protect your feet from injury.

Avoiding injuries from tools

More cutting and piercing injuries occur in the garden than anywhere else in the home except in the kitchen. The main culprit is the lawn-mower, followed by hedgetrimmers, spades, forks and secateurs. If you work with these tools regularly, have a tetanus jab as a precaution.

● All **bladed tools** are potentially dangerous, and powered tools especially so. Never put your fingers anywhere near the blades of a power lawn-mower, a hedgetrimmer, a lawn trimmer or a garden shredder when the motor is running, and allow time for the blades to come to a standstill after switching off the motor. Unplug electrical tools and immobilise petrol-driven ones (by disconnecting the spark plug) before freeing jammed blades, clearing trapped material or cleaning the tool.

● Mind your feet when using a **spade or fork**, especially when deep-digging in rough ground.

● Cut away from your body when using **knives** and similar tools, and keep the fingers of your free hand out of the way when pruning with **secateurs**.

● When using a **mains-powered tool**, always plug it into either a socket outlet containing a residual current device (RCD) or into an RCD adaptor, so that you will be protected from accidental contact with live parts. Make sure that the flex is clearly visible at all times (white or orange flex is far preferable to black, especially if an extension lead is used). If you need an extension lead, use weatherproof rubber two-part connectors fitted on the flex close to the appliance to connect the lead to it, and double-check that the part with the pins is on the appliance flex, the part with the mating sockets on the extension lead. Never use a mains-powered tool out of doors in wet conditions.

● When cutting grass with an **electric lawn-mower**, keep the flex behind you and to one side of the mower's path. When cutting hedges with an **electric hedgetrimmer**, check every time before you switch on the tool that the flex is clear of the blades.

● Use a **chainsaw** only if you have had proper training by a professional: the tool can kick back severely if improperly used, causing horrific injuries. Always wear the appropriate **safety gear** – a safety helmet with integral visor and ear-defenders, safety gauntlets and ideally a special safety jacket, over-trousers and protective spats over your footwear. Never use a chainsaw off the ground: it's not just the saw but the branches that are dangerous. Call in a tree surgeon instead.

Avoiding eye injuries

● One of the commonest eye injuries is caused by bending over an **unseen garden cane**. Guard against this by fitting all canes with brightly coloured rubber or plastic caps; upturned yogurt pots are a tolerable if rather ugly substitute.
● It is a good idea to wear safety spectacles or goggles when using a **rotary mower or lawn trimmer** to protect your eyes from the risk of injury from flying stone chips or other debris.

Avoiding collisions

Collisions in the garden are something of an occupational hazard for adults at work and for children at play. In general terms, it pays to remove potential hazards such as branches at head height, and to take care over the positioning of things like hanging baskets. For children, the biggest danger comes from garden play equipment, especially swings and slides.

● Make sure that **swing seats** have really well-padded edges, and that the swing frame is securely fixed to the ground.
● Minimise the dangers of falls from **play equipment** by excavating the area around it to a depth of about 100mm (4in) and filling the excavation with bark chippings, retained by pegged boards around the perimeter. The chippings are clean, do not blow about too much and provide a cushioned landing that lessens the risk of injury.
● If you have small children, **avoid low planters and free-standing ornaments** such as bird baths and garden gnomes. They may not seem a danger to you, but are at just the right height to

injure a child who is not looking where he or she is going. If you must have a bird-bath or other similar ornament, secure the heavy top section to make it impossible for it to be pulled over.

Avoiding accidents with furniture

Items of garden furniture, especially things that fold up for storage, cause a surprisingly large number of injuries every year. These are mainly falls due to the furniture not being set up or adjusted properly, and injuries to hands (and occasionally feet or other parts of the anatomy) that are trapped in the folding mechanism.

Always take care to set up such furniture carefully and check that moving parts are fully extended, interlocked or braced, as appropriate.

- Do not try to adjust **chairs or sun-beds** when using them. Get up, and check that the moving parts are properly engaged before sitting or lying down again.
- **Check the condition of all garden furniture** at the start and end of every season. Look particularly for splits and tears in fabric covers and for loose components of joints in the frame. Repair or replace any faulty furniture before it can injure someone.

Avoiding accidents with water

If you have small children and a garden pond or swimming-pool, or your children use a paddling-pool, be alert to the dangers of water: a child can drown in seconds in as little as 75mm (3in) of water.

- Keep small children away from a **garden pond** at all times unless they are supervised. Fence around it if you cannot guarantee the supervision.
- Keep a constant eye on children using a **paddling-pool**. Empty the pool every time it is finished with and deflate it or leave it upturned; rainwater can collect in it otherwise, creating a hazard you may not notice.
- Always **supervise swimming sessions** involving children. If you have toddlers, install a fence with a secure gate around the pool.

Avoiding accidents with chemicals

Many garden chemicals are potentially harmful, especially weed-killers. They mainly injure children, but adults are not immune. Pets can be at risk too.

● Always **read the instructions for use** carefully, noting any safety precautions recommended, and follow them to the letter.
● **Store chemicals out of sight** and reach of children, ideally under lock and key. Never transfer chemicals to unmarked containers.
● If using **chemicals that need diluting or dissolving** in water, make up only as much as you need for the job. Wash containers out carefully afterwards.
● Never spray **weedkillers**, but use a watering can. Do not apply pesticides at all in breezy weather. Always wear safety goggles.

Avoiding poisonous and irritant plants

Remember that natural chemicals in some garden plants − especially their berries − can be dangerous. See opposite for a list of plants that are toxic or otherwise harmful. Watch out also for mushrooms and other fungi, which can appear overnight, and teach your children never to touch them.

Avoiding accidents with fire

There are two common causes of injury from fire in the garden − bonfires and barbecues − and every November around 1,000 more injuries are reported as a result of accidents with fireworks.

● If you must have a **bonfire** (composting garden rubbish is a much 'greener' solution to the problem of garden rubbish), site it well away from trees, hedges, sheds, fences and the house. Burn only dry material in a proper incinerator to minimise the amount of smoke produced. Never use petrol, paraffin or other flammable liquid to get the fire going. Supervise it continuously, with the

[continues on page 44]

Toxic plants

The plants listed below are harmful if eaten, and some may also cause skin allergies in some people. If you have children, or if children regularly visit your home, make sure that any of the garden plants are at the back of borders, and train children not to eat any plant they do not recognise as a fruit or vegetable.

Botanical name	Common name
Aconitum	Monkshood
Arum*	Lords and ladies
Atropa	Deadly nightshade
Colchicum	Autumn crocus
Convallaria majalis	Lily of the valley
Daphne laureola**	Spurge laurel
Daphne mezereum**	Mezereon
Daphne (all other species)	
Datura†	
Dieffenbachia†*	Dumb cane/leopard lily
Digitalis	Foxglove
Gloriosa superba†	Glory lily
Hyoscyamus	Henbane
Laburnum	
Lantana	
Nerium oleander†	Oleander
Pernettya	
Phytolacca	Poke weed
Ricinus communis	Caster oil plant
Solanum dulcamara	Woody nightshade
Taxus	Yew
Veratrum	False hellebore

* also a skin and eye irritant   ** may also cause a skin allergy
† house or conservatory plant

In addition, *Ruta* (rue) is severely toxic to skin in sunlight, and *Dictamnus albus* (burning bush) can be a skin irritant in sunlight; *Primula obconica*† may cause a skin allergy.

This list conforms with the Horticultural Trades Association voluntary Code of Recommended Retail Practice.

garden hose to hand in case it gets out of control. Do not leave it to smoulder, but douse the embers with water or soil.

● Position **barbecues** well away from fences, sheds and overhanging trees. Use only proprietary firelighters or starter fluid to light the fuel, *never* petrol or other inflammable liquid. Supervise it at all times, and douse it with soil or sand when you have finished cooking.

● **Follow the firework code.** Keep fireworks in a closed metal container; light them singly yourself (children should never be allowed to light fireworks), with each one at arm's length. Keep away once the firework is lit (and if it fails to light), and have a bucket of water handy for emergencies. Keep all pets indoors.

D-i-y safety

Do-it-yourself is not an inherently dangerous activity, yet almost 90,000 people need hospital treatment every year for injuries sustained while doing it, and many thousands more patch themselves up at home. More tragically, some 70 people kill themselves each year, although these deaths are mainly the result of falls while carrying out d-i-y jobs rather than being caused by the job itself.

The trouble is that few householders are qualified decorators, builders, roofers, plumbers or electricians, although the d-i-y industry tries to convince them that they are. It bombards them with new tools and materials that claim to be easier than ever to use, and provides an endless stream of books, magazines and videos that exhort them to try jobs they might otherwise never dream of undertaking. So d-i-yers try them, often blissfully unaware of the potential dangers that the professional learned about on the first day of his or her apprenticeship.

However, this is seldom the manufacturer's fault. D-i-y tools need sharp blades and powerful motors, and many d-i-y products by their very nature contain potentially harmful ingredients. The main problem is that people do not like reading the instructions that every responsible manufacturer provides, and as a result they do not use things properly.

The other factor that contributes to many d-i-y accidents is carelessness – recklessness, even. Every d-i-yer has hit a thumb with a wayward hammer or cut a finger on a sharp blade, and many more have been badly hurt as a result of a moment's inattention or the taking of an unnecessary chance when doing a job they started tackling for pleasure. 'He did it himself' is a gruesomely fitting epitaph for the risk-taker.

Avoiding falls

More deaths and serious injuries are caused by falls than by any other d-i-y activity, yet many people persist in using access equipment improperly and without taking obvious safety precautions. The golden rule is to use the right equipment for the job, and to use it properly. Improvisation usually spells disaster.

● **Always set up ladders at the correct angle**. It's best if you have someone to assist you. Position the bottom of the ladder 1m away from the base of the wall for every 4m of ladder height. If you set it up too steeply you may overbalance backwards as you climb, and you will probably damage the ladder or find its base slipping away if you try to use it at too shallow an angle. If possible, tie the top of the ladder to the building, and ensure that the bottom is either standing on firm, level ground or is resting on a stout board that is securely packed underneath so it is itself level.

● **Never climb a ladder with your hands full**. Wear a tool belt or apron, haul up the things you need using a rope and bucket after climbing the ladder, or get someone to pass them to you through a nearby window.

● **Do not be tempted to lean out too far**; you may lose your balance and fall, or cause the ladder to slide sideways across the face of the wall. Keep your hips within the line of the ladder stiles, and keep hold of the ladder with one hand whenever possible.

● If you have a **wooden ladder**, store it under cover. Check its condition every time you use it to ensure that the rungs and stiles are sound and free from rot. Do not paint a wooden ladder, since this may conceal potentially dangerous defects.

● **Slot-together platform towers** are generally safer than ladders, but must also be set up on level ground and should be securely tied to the building if they are more than about 4m (13ft) tall. When using one, always fit a handrail and toe boards around the work platform (the boards stop tools and other objects being accidentally knocked off the platform). Never climb the outside of the tower itself. If you use a ladder for access to the platform instead of climbing up the inside of the tower, rest it against the side furthest away from the house wall; the tower may topple over otherwise.

Avoiding accidents with tools

Tools with sharp blades are inherently dangerous, and every year thousands of people cut themselves – often quite badly – with knives, chisels, saws and so on, usually as a result of using them without due care. Power tools are by and large safe but saws and routers in particular need very careful handling.

- **Use the correct tool for the job** and ask yourself whether you are competent to use it. Make sure the piece you are working on is secure.
- When using a **bladed tool**, always make sure that your hands are behind the cutting direction and out of the cutting line. Take special care when using trimming knives; they cause more cuts than any other tool.
- **Keep bladed tools sharp**: ironically, you are more likely to have an accident with a blunt tool than with a sharp one, because you have to use force to make it cut properly.
- **Store bladed tools and spare blades carefully**, both to protect the tools themselves and also to avoid cutting your hands when picking them up. Fit blade guards whenever possible.
- When using a **power tool** for the first time, always read the operating and safety instructions provided so you know what the possible dangers are. Never try to bypass or deactivate any safety guard fitted to the tool. Avoid wearing loose-fitting clothing that could be caught up by fast-moving parts, tie back long hair, and wear appropriate personal protection equipment.

Avoiding accidents with d-i-y materials

The huge range of d-i-y liquids and powders includes some materials – paint strippers, adhesives, wood preservatives and the like – that are clearly dangerous if not used with care. They may burn skin, injure eyes or give off unpleasant or inflammable fumes. You may also use materials that seem relatively innocuous but which can be irritating to handle: cement powder and glass-fibre insulation materials are two obvious contenders. You should also be on the lookout for any old building materials or surfaces that could contain asbestos, such as rigid roofing sheets and old textured ceiling coatings.

● Always **read carefully the instructions** on the packaging before using any d-i-y product, in particular any relating to specific first-aid action to be taken if an accident occurs. Keep separately packaged instruction leaflets safely in a file for future reference. If the print is too small for you to read clearly – a problem especially with many adhesives – complain to the manufacturer and don't buy the product.

● Wear the **appropriate safety equipment** to protect your eyes, ears, lungs, hands and feet; see Avoiding secondary dangers below for more details.

● If you have to work with old materials which may contain **asbestos**, take care to avoid creating dust which you might inhale. Soak the surface with water before trying to cut, drill or abrade it, and bag up damp dust and off-cuts securely. Never dispose of such materials with ordinary household waste; instead, contact your local authority for advice. See page 65 for more details.

Avoiding secondary dangers

Many d-i-y activities generate their own hazards – dust, noise, flying or falling debris, heat and fumes, for example. They are hard to avoid, but you can at least take steps to minimise their effects by using the appropriate safety equipment. Apart from protective footwear (see below), everything you need is both widely available and relatively inexpensive.

● Wear **safety goggles or spectacles** made to British Standard BS2092 to guard against eye injuries when tackling jobs, such as drilling and sawing, driving masonry nails or using splashy chemicals.

● Wear a **disposable face mask** (or one with a disposable filter) so that you do not inhale the relatively coarse but non-toxic airborne dust created by many drilling, sawing and sanding jobs. To protect youself from vapour (when spray-painting your car, for example) or from toxic dust, you will need a specialist mask made to BS2091 or BS EN 149:1992.

- Wear **ear-defenders or ear-plugs** made to BS6344 to protect your hearing during especially noisy jobs, such as sanding a floor or using a concrete breaker in a confined space.
- Use **leather gloves** for general wear and for handling coarse building materials, and PVC gloves when working with chemicals that could harm the skin.
- Wear a **safety helmet** made to BS5240 to protect your head during jobs such as demolition work, or when working on scaffolding. If you are bald or thinning on top, a simple cap will protect your scalp from minor knocks during other d-i-y jobs.
- Wear **protective footwear** (made to BS1870 for men, BS4972 for women) to save your feet from injury caused by dropped heavy objects or moving blades. Such footwear is not widely available; look under Industrial protective clothing in your local *Yellow Pages* for suppliers in your area.
- Wear **warm clothes** if working outside in the cold.

Avoiding electric shocks

Everyone knows that electricity can kill, but many d-i-yers nevertheless take chances when working on their electrical installation. The cardinal rule is always to switch off the power before starting work.

- **Do not tackle electrical work** unless you know exactly what you are doing and are confident of your ability to complete the job to professional standards.
- Guard against the risk of hitting a hidden electric cable (or a water pipe) by using a **battery-powered cable detector**.
- Always plug **power tools being used out of doors** into a special socket outlet or an adaptor containing a residual current device (RCD). This will cut off the power supply in certain potentially dangerous circumstances, and could save your life.

Avoiding unnecessary risks

The key to avoiding d-i-y accidents is to think ahead throughout the job, to concentrate on what you are doing and to be on the lookout for possible danger at all times.

- **Plan each job carefully,** so you have all the right equipment and materials available and will not have to improvise or take short cuts – both recipes for disaster.
- Make sure you know how to carry out the job you are tackling by **doing your homework** thoroughly first.
- **Work within your capabilities,** avoiding dangerous manoeuvres such as overreaching from ladders or trying to lift heavy objects.

Fire

Every year there are about 60,000 major house fires to which the fire brigade is called, and many thousands more minor incidents that escape the official statistics. Every year several hundred men, women and children die as a result, many of them trapped because they discovered the fire too late. Cooking appliances start the most fires, but they are rarely fatal; fires started by smokers' materials and fumes from burning furnishings account for most of the deaths, and night-time is the biggest danger period.

There are five main precautions you can take to make your home safe from the danger of fire and to protect its occupants. They are:

- eliminate fire hazards
- fit smoke detectors
- keep basic fire-fighting equipment in high-risk areas
- learn what to do if a fire breaks out
- make sure that every member of the family knows how to get out of the house quickly and safely.

Avoiding fire hazards

Every home contains its fair share of fire hazards, many of them unrecognised as such. Use this list to check your home so you can eliminate any you find and take whatever action is needed to improve the safety of your home.

Electrical hazards
Electricity starts house fires in two ways: by overheating some part of

the wiring system or by igniting something that comes into contact with a heating element.

- **Do not overload socket outlets**, either mechanically with adaptors or electrically by plugging in too many high-wattage appliances.
- **Have your wiring tested** by a qualified electrician if it is more than about 20 years old or if you detect the tell-tale fishy smell of overheating cable or wiring accessories.
- Even though it is a statutory requirement for **electric blankets** to be BEAB-approved, have them checked by the manufacturer every three to four years. Always turn underblankets off when you get into bed.
- If you do not have a **residual current device** (RCD) fitted at your consumer unit or fusebox to protect the property from the risk of fire started by an electrical fault, get a professional electrician to install one.

Kitchen hazards

Most fires in the kitchen are caused by careless use of the cooker, especially the hob, or by drying clothes using electric heaters.

- Never leave a **chip pan** unattended or attempt to move it when it is hot. If you must fry chips, buy a thermostatically controlled deep-fat fryer instead. Keep a **fire-blanket** (made to British Standard BS6575) on the kitchen wall in case a pan does catch fire.
- Do not dry **tea-towels** on plate racks or eye-level grills; they could fall or be blown on to a still-hot hob.
- Do not run **washing-machines or dishwashers** overnight; if you must, install a linked smoke alarm nearby.

Heater hazards

Heating equipment, especially open or radiant fires, can be dangerous if left unattended or used in an improper manner.

- Always place a **fire-guard** in front of an unattended open fire, particularly at bedtime. If the fire is still burning then, make sure no flammable items such as log baskets are close to the grate, where they could overheat and ignite. If there are small children in the family, fix the fire-guard in place with child-resistant catches so that they cannot remove it.

- Avoid siting a **mirror** above an open fire, because of the risk of clothing catching fire when someone uses it.
- Never use an electric heater to help **dry clothes**. A radiant element will quickly start a fire, while a convector heater will soon overheat if its air inlet or outlet grilles are blocked.
- Do not use time-switches to control radiant heaters: they could come on unexpectedly and start a fire if close to inflammable materials.

Furniture hazards

Fumes from burning textiles, upholstery or furnishings are responsible for more deaths than the fire's flames. Items upholstered with plastic foam are the biggest culprits.

- Replace old **foam-filled furniture** at the earliest possible opportunity with items labelled to indicate that the covers and fillings meet the requirements of the Furniture and Furnishings (Fire) (Safety) Regulations 1988. The regulations apply to beds and mattresses and to the fillings of pillows and cushions as well as to living-room furniture.
- Have **older at-risk furnishings** professionally treated with fire-retardant chemicals; curtains can also be treated in this way.

Smoking hazards

Smokers' materials and matches are responsible for starting roughly one in six major fires, but cause around a third of all fire deaths.

- Always use an **ashtray** when 'resting' a cigarette, ideally one without side rests from which it can easily fall if it is left to burn down unattended. Ensure that all butts are completely extinguished before emptying ashtrays into rubbish bins.
- Never smoke in **bed**.
- Keep all smokers' materials out of the sight and reach of **children** at all times.

Storage hazards

Be on the alert for materials stored around the house which could help to fuel a fire.

- Do not store **old newspapers** or other easily ignitable materials under the stairs, where they could cause the staircase to catch fire and block your primary escape route.
- Store **aerosols and flammable liquids** away from any source of heat. Never store petrol inside the house.

Escape hazards

It is vital that your way out of the house in the event of a fire is not unduly obstructed.

- Make sure that the **keys for window and door locks** are accessible – not in place in the lock, which some insurance companies forbid, but close by.
- Make sure that **windows open easily**. Every bedroom should have an opening casement; a room with sealed-unit double glazing and only an opening top light could be a potential death-trap.

Smoke detectors

All new homes must now by law have mains-powered smoke detectors installed. Every other home in the land should have at least one battery- or mains-powered detector, and the Home Office estimates that around two-thirds of homes now do so. Your chances of surviving a fire are increased twofold or threefold if you have one because the warning gives you more time to escape.

Basic battery-powered detectors cost relatively little, and mains-powered types are not much dearer. All have a test button so that you can check that they are working, and most battery-powered ones also have a low-battery warning indicator. Many can be inter-connected so that if one detects smoke, it causes others linked to it to sound as well. Some feature a bright escape light that comes on when the alarm sounds. Make sure that any you buy carry the British Standard Kitemark and meet British Standard BS5446.

If you install only one detector, the best place to fit it is to the hall ceiling, above the foot of the stairs. Keep ceiling-mounted detectors at least 300mm (12in) away from a wall or light fitting, and position wall-mounted ones between 150 and 300mm (6 to 12in) below ceiling level. If you want a second detector, fit it on the landing. Add further detectors in bedrooms occupied by children or elderly people, and in integral garages. Do not put one in the kitchen: cooking can cause nuisance tripping of the detector. However, it is worth having one if you regularly run washing machines or dishwashers unattended overnight; both machines have been known to start fires due to electrical faults.

Test smoke detectors regularly – at least once a month – by operating the test button. This ensures that the electronics are in working order. To check its response to real smoke, snuff a match out under it or blow cigarette smoke into it. Do this once a year; more frequent testing could leave smoke deposits which could reduce the detector's sensitivity. Finally, replace the battery regularly once a year – on a day you won't forget, such as your birthday.

Fire-fighting equipment

The only fire-fighting equipment that every home ought to have is a fire-blanket, which should be kept in the kitchen – close to but not above the hob, where most kitchen fires start. Buy one that meets British Standard BS6575.

Fire-extinguishers for home use are widely available, but are not generally recommended by fire-prevention experts, except as a safeguard if you live a long way from your nearest fire station. If you decide you do want one, ask your local fire brigade's fire prevention officer for advice on which to buy and find out where you can get it serviced regularly to ensure that it is always in perfect working order.

Tackling fires yourself

If you start a fire or discover one during the day, you must make a snap decision about whether to tackle it yourself or get out of the house and call the fire brigade. Tackling a small fire yourself may minimise the damage caused, but it is an option you should take only if you will not put yourself or anyone else at risk.

● For **chip pan and frying pan fires**, turn off the heat source. Then cover the pan with a fire-blanket if you have one, a damp towel otherwise, to put out the flames. Do not try to move the pan; leave it to cool down for at least 30 minutes. *Never* throw water on to a burning pan of oil.

- If **foam-filled furniture** catches fire, do not waste time trying to put it out; the fumes can kill within a minute or so. Get everyone else out of the house, close the door and call the fire brigade immediately. Then wait outside the house until the fire engine arrives.
- If an **electrical appliance** is involved, unplug the appliance, if possible; otherwise turn off the power at the fusebox or consumer unit. Only when the power is disconnected should you douse the flames with water or a fire-extinguisher. Unplug TVs or computers and cover them with a damp towel or a fire-blanket to smother the fire – *do not use water*.
- If an **oil heater** catches fire, douse it with buckets of water thrown over it from a safe distance.
- If **clothes** catch fire, lay the victim down so that the flames cannot reach the face and either douse them with water or any non-flammable liquid you have to hand, or smother the flames with a blanket or rug if one is readily available. Depending on the extent of the burns, take the victim to a hospital casualty department or ring for an ambulance. See also page 191.

Fire drill

Make sure everyone in the family knows what to do if a fire does start, especially at night. Here are the rules.

- If you **smell smoke at night**, wake everyone immediately and try to establish where the seat of the fire is so you can work out what to do.
- **Close the door** to the room where the fire is if you can; this will help to starve it of oxygen. If you have to open a door to seek the source of the fire, check whether it feels warm to the touch first and leave it closed if it does.
- **Use the stairs if visibility permits** and they are safe to use, and get everyone out of the house.
- **Wake a neighbour** to call the fire brigade. Give the address slowly and clearly, and tell them if people are trapped in the building. Do not attempt to rescue them yourself.
- **Under no circumstances** should you return to the house to save possessions or pets.

- If escape via the stairs is blocked, use an upstairs window as an **escape route** if possible. Otherwise go to a front bedroom, close the door and seal round it with bedding or clothes. Then open a window and call for help.
- Jump from a first-floor window only as a **last resort**, lowering yourself feet first from the window sill to reduce the height of the drop. Try to land with your knees bent, and crumple as you hit the ground so that your body absorbs the impact. Then encourage others to do the same. Get an adult to suspend small children from the window by their arms, so you can reach up and catch them as they fall. In buildings of more than two storeys, wait for the fire brigade to arrive; you will be badly injured or even killed jumping from such a height.

Safe practices

Lastly, there are several common-sense things you can do to give you greater peace of mind about fire safety in your home.

- **Close room doors downstairs** before retiring for the night. This will help contain a fire if one breaks out.
- Make sure that any still-burning **open fires are properly guarded**, and turn off radiant or convector heaters. Double-check that all smoking materials are safely extinguished.
- Since fires often start at night and most homes have only one flight of stairs, which may in any case be alight, work out in advance possible **means of escape from upstairs windows** – ideally, one opening on to a flat roof; otherwise one with a flower-bed or lawn below it rather than a hard surface.
- Make sure that visitors staying in your home know what your **smoke detector** sounds like and what your pre-planned escape route is.

Gas and electricity

Neither mains nor bottled gas will poison you, but both can explode if they leak and can kill if not burned properly in a fire, boiler or other appliance. Electricity, on the other hand, is lethal if it is not used safely or treated with respect. Thankfully, deaths resulting from gas leaks or electrocution are relatively rare, but even one accidental death is one too many.

Using gas safely

Gas is a perfectly safe fuel so long as it is used correctly. Following these safety guidelines will ensure that no one in your home is put at risk.

● Always buy appliances that comply with either **British or European Standards**. Gas showrooms sell only approved appliances.
● Have all gas appliances **installed by a qualified fitter** – either a British Gas employee or a member of CORGI (the Council for Registered Gas Installers*).
● Have gas appliances **serviced regularly** – at least annually – either under a British Gas service contract or by a CORGI-registered firm, to ensure that they are working safely and efficiently.
● Call the gas emergency number if you suspect that any gas appliance is **faulty**, and stop using it until you have had it checked by an expert.
● Ensure that rooms containing gas-burning appliances are **properly ventilated** (balanced-flue appliances such as boilers take their air supply directly from outside). If you get headaches or nausea when an appliance is on, it may not be burning properly and may be producing potentially lethal carbon monoxide (CO) gas. The room should have trickle ventilators above the windows and an airbrick in an outside wall or a floor grille if the floor is suspended, and these should not be closed or covered at any time. CO can still build up if these ventilation openings are too small for the appliance being used in the room. Have conventional flues checked regularly for partial blockages – ideally when the appliance is serviced.
● Consider having an **electric gas detector** installed – ideally a mains-powered type made to British Standard BS7348. Have it wired up permanently to a fused connection unit rather than plugged into a socket outlet, since unplugging it could cause a spark and an explosion if a gas leak occurs. There are different types for natural and bottled gas, and each must be installed correctly – high on a wall to detect the lighter-than-air methane

in natural gas and low down for the heavier-than-air propane and butane in bottled gas. These do not detect the presence of CO gas.

- If you have **gas heaters in bedrooms** which may be running while you or your family are asleep, a CO detector will give additional peace of mind. This works in a similar way to a smoke detector, sounding an alarm if CO is present.

- **Do not attempt to carry out any d-i-y work** involving gas pipes, fittings or appliances: it is against the law. Always leave the job to a qualified gas fitter. If you have gas appliances that are not linked to their supply by a modern bayonet-type connector, get them converted.

Coping with a gas leak

It is essential that you and your family know what to do if anyone detects a strong smell of gas in the house.

- **Turn off the gas tap** next to the gas meter by rotating the lever to a position at right angles to the pipework. With bottled gas supplies, turn off the main valve on the cylinder or supply pipe.

- **Open doors and windows** to disperse the gas as quickly as possible.

- **Put out all naked lights**, and extinguish cigarettes with water.

- Do not operate any **electrical switches** – even a doorbell – since this could cause a spark. Leave everything as it is, on or off.

- Check whether **pilot lights** on cookers and boilers are lit, and whether controls on cookers or gas fires have been left on without the burners being lit. Relight pilot lights only when the smell of gas has disappeared.

- **If the smell of gas persists**, call your local gas emergency telephone number immediately; you will find it listed under Gas in your telephone directory. British Gas must by law make a leak safe within 12 hours of being notified.

Using bottled gas

If you use LPG (liquefied petroleum gas) either from an outdoor tank or in smaller cylinders and cartridges for individual heaters and other appliances, even a small leak can produce a large amount of highly flammable gas. If this ignites, the result can be a fierce fire or an explosion.

- Make sure that appliances using LPG have **adequate ventilation**, and that connecting hoses are free from signs of cracking or perishing. Test hoses and connections for leaks by applying soapy water; a leak will create tell-tale bubbles.
- Always change LPG cylinders and cartridges **in the open air** if possible. Do not smoke when doing so, and extinguish naked lights in the vicinity. Beware of sparks from electrical tools, too.
- **Store spare cylinders and cartridges** outside the house above ground level so that gas cannot accumulate in hollows – in a well-ventilated outbuilding would be ideal. Keep them upright. Lock them up if you have children in the family.

Using electricity safely

There are several common-sense points to remember about your everyday use of electricity, and a number of rules to obey if you do your own electrical wiring work. Follow them, and electric shocks or worse should never happen in your home … but be prepared, just in case, and make sure you know what action to take.

Everyday safety

- **Keep water and electricity well apart**. Do not operate switches or plug in appliances with wet hands. If a portable appliance or its plug gets wet, allow it to dry out thoroughly before using it. Turn off the power at the main switch before washing down walls or stripping wallpaper, and check that wall switches and socket outlets are dry inside before restoring the power. Never take an electrical appliance into a bathroom, even if the flex is long enough. Do not use electrical equipment out of doors in wet conditions.
- **Do not overload socket outlets or power circuits** by plugging in too many high-powered appliances. Avoid the use of adaptors; have more outlets installed instead.
- **Avoid long trailing flexes** if you can, and tuck any that you have out of the way behind furniture so they are not a trip hazard. Fit short or curly flexes to portable appliances used in the kitchen. Check the condition of appliance flexes regularly, and repair or replace any that are frayed or damaged.
- **Regularly inspect appliance plugs** (approved to BS1363) to

ensure that they are undamaged, firmly closed and properly connected inside, with tight terminal screws, working flex grips and a fuse of the correct rating – 3-amp for appliances rated at less than 690 watts and 13-amp otherwise.

● If using an **extension lead**, always uncoil it fully from its drum; it could overheat and catch fire otherwise. Check that its flex rating is suitable for the appliance it is supplying, especially if this is a heater.

● Always unplug an electrical appliance from the mains before **cleaning** it, fitting replaceable components or attempting to trace an electrical fault.

● Always turn the electricity supply off at the mains before attempting to **replace a blown rewirable or cartridge fuse**. Fit new fuse wire or a replacement cartridge fuse of the correct rating for the circuit concerned – 5 amps for lighting circuits, 15 amps for immersion heaters and 30 (or occasionally 20) amps for power circuits. Replace the cover over the fuseholders before restoring the power. *Never* replace a blown fuse with any other metallic object; the circuit will have no overload protection and someone could be killed by your stupidity.

● Always use a residual current device (RCD) whenever working with **portable tools or other appliances out of doors**. You can plug them into a special socket outlet containing an RCD if your home has one (all new homes must), or use an RCD adaptor otherwise. Use the RCD test button regularly to check its operation.

Safety with wiring work

The legal situation regarding d-i-y electrical work in the UK is unusual. In many other countries licensed electricians must carry out – or at least supervise – the work. Here, except in Scotland (where electrical systems are covered by the Scottish Building Regulations which have the force of law), anyone can carry out wiring work without any legal restriction or any statutory guidelines to follow. The only potential restraint lies with local electricity companies, which have the right to test domestic wiring work for safety and to refuse to supply an unsafe installation.

In the absence of any legal guidelines, any d-i-y electrical work you carry out should instead comply with the Regulations for

Electrical Installations, drawn up by the Institution of Electrical Engineers (IEE)★ and used by all professional electricians. They are generally referred to as the IEE Wiring Regulations and are revised regularly. The current edition is the sixteenth; it was made into a British Standard (BS7671) in 1992.

- Do not carry out any work on your **house wiring** unless you are confident that you know what you are doing and can complete the job safely and correctly. Otherwise, always use a qualified electrician – a member of the Electrical Contractors' Association (ECA)★ or the Electrical Contractors' Association of Scotland★, or on the roll of the National Inspection Council for Electrical Installation Contracting (NICEIC)★. You can get names of qualified people working in your area from these bodies or from your local electricity company showroom.

- Always turn off the power supply at the main isolator switch or whole-house residual current device (RCD) **before working on your home's wiring system**. If you are working on just one circuit, remove the circuit fuse and restore the power to the other circuits, or switch off the circuit's miniature circuit breaker (MCB). Take care when working on two-way switching arrangements, which can (but should not) link two lighting circuits.

- Always **double-check all connections inside wiring accessories** to ensure that the cable cores are linked to the correct terminals and are securely held by the terminal screws.

- **Never omit the earth connection**. The only circumstances where one is not needed is in the flex run to a non-metallic lampholder and to double-insulated power tools or electrical appliances.

- **Have all major rewiring work checked** by a qualified electrician.

Shock treatment

If an appliance or a wiring accessory gives you (or anyone else) a minor shock, stop using it at once. Have the appliance checked by an appliance repair expert for earth safety, and replace the wiring accessory if it is damaged and live parts are exposed.

See page 192 for how to give the correct first aid treatment.

Glass

Glass is an ideal material for a variety of things in the home – drinking vessels, ornaments, shelves, mirrors, light bulbs and, of course, the glazing in windows and doors. However, it has one major drawback as far as home safety is concerned: if it breaks, the resulting fragments can be razor-sharp and can inflict severe, even fatal, cuts to soft tissue. Preventing accidents with everyday glass objects is largely down to a combination of care and common sense; guarding against accidents with fixed glass means replacing it with safety glass in individual danger areas.

Everyday safety

The only certain way to avoid everyday accidents with glass is to banish it from your home as far as possible. This is especially advisable if you have small children, and applies also to the homes of elderly or disabled people. Follow these guidelines:

- Use **plastic drinking glasses**, and buy household and cosmetic products only in plastic containers – especially for use in the bathroom.
- Display **glass ornaments** in closed – and ideally locked – cabinets rather than on open shelving, tables and the like.
- **Avoid using glass shelves** if possible, especially in the bathroom. If you must have them, use glass at least 6mm ('/4in) thick, have the edges rounded and polished, and make sure they are securely held by their brackets. Glass table-tops and glazed cabinet doors are also a potential danger; choose solid tables and doors wherever possible.
- Make sure that **mirrors and glazed pictures are securely hung**. Pin-type picture hooks are unsuitable for items weighing more than about 1kg (2.2lbs); use screw-in fixings for heavier items. Mirrors are best hung using proprietary support clips; framed types are safer than unframed ones, even if they have bevelled and polished edges.
- Use **light fittings** that enclose and protect the bulb if possible. Always use a cloth to grip the bulb when changing it, especially if it is hot. This will also protect your hand if the glass breaks. Fit

energy-saving bulbs with toughened glass in exposed locations where the bulb might be broken accidentally.

Safety glazing

The current Building Regulations contain, for the first time, requirements for controlling the use of fixed glass in buildings. They were introduced (rather belatedly) to try to reduce the number of serious injuries resulting from people falling against or colliding with glass panes in windows and doors. Although they apply only to new buildings, you should consider implementing their requirements in your home if you have small children or elderly people – the age-groups most at risk – in the family. You will also have to satisfy the regulations if you are adding a conservatory to your home, even though the building itself will be exempt from Building Regulations control.

The basic requirement is that glazing in certain critical locations must be safe. These areas are:

● **glass in doors** and in **glazed side panels next to doors**, up to a height of 1500mm (4ft 11in) above floor level and up to a distance of 300mm (12in) from the edges of the door opening;

● **glass panels in internal walls and partitions** within 800mm (2ft 8in) of floor level.

To be safe, these areas must be glazed with toughened or laminated glass or with robust glazing materials such as polycarbonate or, for screens, glass blocks. Suitable flat glass and plastic sheet should be made to British Standard BS6206. Small panes in doors and glazed panels can be of ordinary glass so long as it is at least 6mm (¼in) thick, is held in place by glazing beads, has a maximum width of 250mm (10in) and a maximum area of 0.5sq m (just under 5½sq ft). Although not covered by the Building Regulations, shower screens and cubicles should always be of safety glass or equivalent plastic sheet.

An alternative to replacing glass in these critical locations is to fix a permanent screen in front of the glass, to a minimum height of 800mm (31in) and with verticals spaced so the gaps between them are no wider than 75mm (3in) and of a design that is difficult for children to climb.

If replacing glass in vulnerable areas or erecting screens is beyond your budget, there are two other steps you can take to make large areas of glazing safer in your home. The first is to stick on something – bands of coloured adhesive tape, children's peel-and-stick plastic figures or strips of translucent sticky-back plastic – at eye level to warn people of the presence of the glass. The second is to cover the glass with special plastic safety film; you can do this yourself with d-i-y films or have it applied professionally. Incidentally, this improves home security as well as home safety by making the glass more difficult for a would-be burglar to break.

Avoid the use of glass – even wired glass – altogether as a roofing material for structures such as conservatories, porches and covered walkways. Twin- or triple-wall polycarbonate sheeting is safer and lighter in weight, and also has far better insulating properties than a single layer of glass.

Chemicals and hazardous waste

We use scores of chemicals in our homes, and many of them are potentially harmful to people using them, to the environment or to both. Some chemicals can kill, especially if they get into the hands of young children. It is therefore essential that you are aware of the hazards they pose, and how to reduce the risks of using them.

We also create huge amounts of rubbish in our daily lives – over a third of a tonne per person per year. Much of it simply goes in the bin and is carted away by the dustman, although separate collection and subsequent recycling of materials such as glass, paper and the steel and aluminium in cans is now becoming more widespread. However, gardening, d-i-y and car maintenance can all create waste which should not (or cannot) be disposed of in the dustbin because it is potentially hazardous. Getting rid of it safely is essential.

Chemical hazards

Certain categories of hazardous material are defined by law, and any product containing them must name them on the packaging, carry the appropriate warning symbol and give advice on how to use them safely. Those most likely to be found in the home or garden fall into three of these categories: flammable, harmful or irritant, and corrosive.

Common **flammable products** used in the home and garden include methylated spirits, white spirit, solvent-based adhesives, paints, wood stains and wood preservatives, aerosols with solvent propellants, and liquefied petroleum gas.

Harmful or irritant chemicals are found in many d-i-y, car maintenance and gardening products; individual reactions to their effects may vary from person to person.

Corrosive chemicals are few and far between, with the exception of caustic soda and some cleaning agents for ovens, car engines and masonry.

Storing chemicals safely

You must store hazardous chemicals securely away from children, pets and the elements.

- Use **child-resistant catches or locks** on cupboard doors in the kitchen, the garage and the garden shed.
- **Never decant such chemicals** into other containers, even if you label them. A child may recognise a familiar bottle or tin, and may not be able to read. You must by law store products containing pesticides in their original containers.
- Keep risks to a minimum by buying products only when you need them, and **buy only as much as you need** for the job. Stored chemicals can deteriorate in time and their instructions may become illegible or lost.

Using chemicals safely

It cannot be stressed how important it is to read the instructions, plus any safety advice, before using any chemical, even if you think you are familiar with it.

- Take special note of **any warnings** about inhaling vapours, avoiding naked lights in the vicinity and maintaining good ventilation.
- **Wear overalls and gloves** when handling corrosive materials, plus safety goggles if there is any risk of the chemical splashing in your face. If working with caustic soda, always add the crystals to water, not the reverse, since considerable heat is generated as the

crystals dissolve. Take special care if using caustic oven cleaners, making sure that your arms are covered as well as your hands.

● Take special care not to get harmful or irritant chemicals **in your eyes or on your skin**.

● **Never leave chemical products unattended** while you work if you have small children or pets. Always place them out of reach at all times.

● Be scrupulous about **cleaning up** after you have finished work, cleaning containers and wiping surfaces so that no traces of the chemical remain which could harm others or cause damage. Make sure that containers are firmly closed and are returned to secure storage.

Clearing the decks

Like most households, your home and its outbuildings probably contain a veritable arsenal of chemical weapons, many of which you have probably had for years and are unlikely ever to use. For safety's sake, sort them out now and dispose of anything but the bare essentials, in particular:

● **products you cannot identify** or which have missing or illegible instructions;

● **products that are obviously several years old**, because many will deteriorate in storage, especially once they have been opened;

● **old garden weedkillers and pesticides**, many of which are likely to contain chemicals that are now banned for amateur use.

If you have more than the occasional bottle, tin or packet to dispose of, do not bin them; nor should you dispose of them down the WC or into the house drains. Instead, contact your local authority waste disposal department for advice. Most will tell you to bring them to their local waste disposal site and hand them in to a member of their staff, but some will collect large quantities of hazardous products.

You should also contact your local authority if you have any waste material you believe may contain asbestos; old roofing sheets are the likeliest candidate, but you may also have old insulation materials and textured ceiling coatings that could contain it. Most authorities operate a free collection service.

Medicines

Medicines are by far the commonest cause of poisoning in the home, accounting for an average of 50,000 incidents and several hundred deaths each year. Most tragically, over 80 per cent of these cases involve children under five years old. The fault is ours, the remedy simple.

- Keep *all* medical products **out of sight and out of reach of children** at all times, preferably in a securely locked cabinet, taking them out only to dispense them and returning them to the cupboard immediately. This applies even to things you may regard as innocuous – cough mixture, vitamins and the like – which can be dangerous if the specified dose is exceeded. Making sure that medicines have child-resistant closures is advice that should be redundant if you keep everything under lock and key, but does provide a second line of defence if you ever slip up.
- You should not have any **medicinal products** in the home – beyond those in a first-aid kit – which you are not currently taking on the advice of a doctor or pharmacist. If you have any, sort them out now and take them to a pharmaceutical chemist for disposal. Never flush medicines or pills down the WC or put them in household rubbish.
- **Always follow the instructions** with any medical product, whether bought over the counter or obtained on prescription. Never exceed the stated dose or frequency of use.
- Never give your own **prescribed medicines or pills** to someone else. Apart from the obvious foolishness of such action, you could be committing an offence under the Misuse of Drugs Act 1971.
- **Elderly people on medication** may need help if they could become confused over their regime, especially if multiple prescriptions are involved. If you have someone like this in your family or are responsible for their care, seek medical advice.

Children

Children are especially at risk of injury or accidental death in the home; every year over a million children visit a hospital accident and emergency unit following a home accident, and many more are treated by their doctors. Sadly, up to 200 die each year.

You can prevent many of these accidents by a combination of increased awareness of the dangers present in the home, careful education of your children, improvements in home safety and the sensible selection of products for their safety in use. Many earlier parts of this book have mentioned child safety; this short section is intended to summarise that information for ease of reference if you have children in your family or often entertain them as visitors.

Why children have accidents

Understanding why children are especially prone to accidental injury in the home will take you a long way towards preventing many of these accidents. For a start, children – particularly the under-fives – have no concept of danger and are often oblivious to their surroundings, becoming deeply absorbed in their own immediate interests. They are often unaware of danger in their environment because of their limited experience, and their small size can be a hazard in itself in a world designed by and for adults. Most crucial of all, they often simply cannot foresee the consequences of their actions, and their natural inquisitiveness can lead them into danger.

Boys, especially those under five, are more likely to be injured than girls. This may be due to their tendency for bravado and horseplay; many accidents are caused by play involving pushing and wrestling which can get out of hand, especially if it is unsupervised.

Avoiding falls

Over 40 per cent of children's injuries are the result of falls. Most involve tripping over, or falling from a higher level such as a bed or pram or out of a pushchair. The most severe injuries result from falls from a great height – a window, the stairs or a balcony. To reduce the risk of children falling, follow these guidelines:

- Try to **keep floors free of toys** and other obstructions that could be tripped over.
- **Do not place babies on tables**, worktops or other furniture from which they could fall easily.
- **Always use a safety harness** when placing a baby or a child in a

high chair, pram or pushchair, or any other item which has harness anchorage points.

- **Avoid placing furniture in front of windows**, where it could be climbed by a small child.
- **Fit child-resistant locks** on all opening windows.
- On stairs, **use a safety gate** to British Standard BS4125 at the top or bottom of the flight, depending on where you want to pen your offspring. Make sure that balustrades are strong, secure and do not have any footholds a child could climb. Horizontal balustrades are a particular hazard. Do not allow children to play on the stairs, and keep the stairs free of obstructions at all times. If you can, fit a low-level handrail for small children to use.

Avoiding collisions

Learning not to bump into things – and keeping an eye open for things bumping into us – are both part of our development as children. It can be a painful process, but one it is difficult to control in the home or garden.

- Try to **think small**. Things that are no obstacle to an adult can be dangerous to a child, especially those with sharp corners or projections.
- **Keep your eyes open** when moving around the house. It is easy to overlook and collide with a small child on the floor.
- **Take care when carrying things**, especially hot food or drinks.
- **Take care with storage**. It is easy for things to fall or be pulled down on to a child.
- **Choose outdoor play equipment with care**, especially those with moving parts, such as swings and seesaws. Fit it according to the manufacturer's instructions. Add extra padding to seat edges and other hard surfaces for additional protection. Site them on grass rather than concrete.

Avoiding cuts

Cutting and piercing injuries make up about a tenth of child accident statistics, and mainly involve accidents with glass. Its increased use in patio doors, low-level glazing and furniture is mainly responsible.

- Ensure that only safety glass to British Standard BS6206 is used in all **replacement doors and windows** you fit or have installed, and also in a conservatory.

- Make large areas of existing glass safer by applying **special plastic safety film** to it. Do this yourself or employ a professional firm.
- If you must have **glass in furniture**, make sure that it contains safety glass; tables and trolleys should be made to BS7376, and other items, including cabinets, shelving systems and mirrors, to BS7449.
- Always **clear up broken glass immediately** and wipe down or vacuum-clean the surface to remove tiny shards or splinters. Dispose of the debris safely.
- **Keep knives** and bladed implements, especially d-i-y and gardening tools, **out of the reach of children**.
- Avoid using **cold frames and cloches** in a garden where young children play.

Avoiding heat-related accidents

Fires in the home are responsible for almost half of all child fatalities each year, but burns and scalds account for only one injury in twenty. Nevertheless, the resulting injury can be severe and its treatment long and painful. About seventy per cent of such injuries happen to children under five.

- **Hot drinks** are frequently to blame, so don't take a hot drink while holding a child. Place unattended cups and mugs well out of the reach of small children.
- Avoid using **tablecloths** which can easily be pulled off by a young child, bringing hot items from the table down with it.
- **Keep pans away from the front of the hob** when cooking.
- **Fit your kettle with a short or curly lead** that will not droop over the edge of the kitchen worktop, or buy a cordless kettle. Keep the kettle – empty when not in use – at the back of the worktop.
- **Test the temperature of bath or shower water** before allowing a child to use it. Keep your domestic hot-water temperature to a maximum of 54°C (130°F) for safety.
- If you have an open fire, always **use a fire-guard**. Make sure it is secured to the fire surround. Check that the fire-guards on radiant heaters cannot be removed by a child.

- **Check the temperature of your oven door** when cooking; keep children away if it is too hot for you to touch for more than a few seconds, or use an oven door cover. If you are replacing a cooker, make sure that the new one has a cool door.

Avoiding poisoning accidents

Over 50,000 children require in-patient or out-patient treatment for poisoning accidents each year, mainly due to the carelessness of their parents.

- Keep all **medicines**, and also household and garden chemicals, **out of sight and out of reach of children**, ideally under lock and key. Choose products sold in child-resistant containers whenever possible.
- **Never decant chemicals** into other containers which a child might recognise as a favourite food or drink.

Avoiding other accidents

Children are adept at discovering new ways of injuring themselves, and it is up to parents to try to be one jump ahead. Three common but unrelated causes of injury are foreign bodies in the eye or ear, accidents in the bath or a garden pool, and family pets (especially dogs). To reduce the possibility of such dangers:

- Check that your **first-aid kit** contains an eyebath and some small tweezers so you can try to tackle foreign bodies promptly. If you cannot see and remove the object easily, however, take the child immediately to a doctor or hospital.
- **Never leave a small child unsupervised in the bath**, playing in a paddling-pool or in a garden with a pond or unguarded swimming-pool.
- If you have a **pet**, teach your children how to handle and play with it safely. Most pets are very tolerant but have their limits and may bite or scratch if hurt or provoked. Make sure that cages, hutches and the like are safe to use, both for the pet and for the children. See pages 77–8 for more details.

Elderly people

The population contains a higher proportion of elderly people than ever before, and the numbers of deaths and injuries among the over-65s as a result of accidents in the home is disproportionately high – around 2,500 deaths (65 per cent of the total) and over 300,000 injuries each year. By far the commonest cause is a fall of one type or another, accounting for two-thirds of the injuries and around four out of every five deaths. Falls result in fractures in one in five injury cases.

Why elderly people have accidents

Many accidents in the home among the over-65s are the result of frailty and poor health. This can lead to problems such as an unsteady gait, poor eyesight, loss of co-ordination or periodic dizziness, any of which can be a contributory factor in an accident. As people get older, they can become less mentally alert and even seriously confused, the latter often made worse by the overdosing (or underdosing) of medication. They are also often unaware of changes in their abilities, and are frequently stubbornly unwilling to admit to any shortcomings or to change their habits even if the problem is pointed out to them.

Avoiding falls

Most falls take place on the level, in bedrooms and living-rooms, but falls on stairs or off furniture are also commonplace.

- Try to ensure that **living areas** do not contain obvious obstacles, and that traffic routes are clear and easy to follow without unnecessary changes of direction.
- Check that **floorcoverings** are sound and secure, especially on stairs and at door thresholds. Patch or replace worn areas. Avoid rugs, especially on polished floor surfaces.
- Ensure that **lighting** is good, especially on stairs and in kitchens. Fit two-way switching on stairs and in bedrooms for convenience. Have a lamp or torch beside the bed to avoid the dangers of moving around in the dark.

- Use **foldaway steps with a handrail** to reach high cupboards, change light bulbs and so on. Never climb on to furniture to do jobs like this.
- Fit a **handrail** at each side of the stairs, and add **grab-rails** elsewhere around the house for additional support. Provide somewhere to sit down in the kitchen and bathroom if dizzy spells are a problem.
- Avoid wearing long trailing **clothing** and poorly fitting **footwear**.
- Reduce the risks of falls on stairs by moving to **single-storey accommodation** if this is possible, or reorganising your home so you can sleep downstairs otherwise.
- Have a **portable alarm** so that you can summon help if you fall and are incapacitated as a result (see page 76 for more information).

Avoiding fire-related accidents

Over 200 elderly people die in house fires each year, often because of their poor mobility, poor sense of smell, carelessness with smokers' materials and misuse of lighting, heating and cooking equipment.

- Install **smoke detectors** in living-rooms and bedrooms occupied by elderly people.
- Take great care when **smoking**. Use a lighter (safer than matches), place ashtrays in all rooms, and extinguish cigarettes carefully so you are sure they are not smouldering, especially when emptying ashtrays into rubbish bins. Try to avoid smoking in bed.
- **Avoid using candles and open fires** if possible.
- Use **electric blankets** correctly, and have them checked by the manufacturer every three or four years. When buying a new blanket, choose one with overheat protection.

Avoiding poisoning accidents

Medicines taken improperly and carbon monoxide produced by inefficient or poorly ventilated fuel-burning appliances are responsible for most poisoning accidents among elderly people.

- Make sure that elderly people are aware of the need to take **medication** as prescribed, and of the dangers of both overdosing and underdosing. Multiple prescriptions can be particularly dangerous. Seek medical advice if you suspect that an elderly person is having trouble with medication.

- Have **fuel-burning appliances** serviced regularly and use them in accordance with the instructions. At the same time have the ventilation checked, and get chimneys and flues swept if necessary.

Avoiding burns and scalds

Over half of all contact burns to adults happen to people aged over sixty-five, and one in four injuries is fatal.

- Place secure guards around **open fires and other radiant heaters**. If possible, switch to safer heating appliances such as convectors, ideally wall-mounted rather than floor-standing.
- Many scalding injuries involve **kettles and spilt drinks**. Jug and cordless electric kettles are safer than those heated on a hob. Make sure a jug kettle has a coiled flex for safety. Avoid carrying hot drinks further than necessary, and set them down where you can reach them easily.
- If using a **hot-water bottle**, do not fill it with boiling water. As soon as it shows any signs of perishing, replace it with a rubber one made to British Standard BS1970 or a plastic one made to BS6728.

Avoiding hypothermia

Hypothermia occurs when the body temperature drops below about 35°C (95°F), and is a contributory factor in causing several hundred deaths among elderly people each year. Its onset can be insidious.

- If you are unable to heat your whole home to an adequate level, **keep one room warm**. Move about at regular intervals to maintain circulation.
- Wear **several thin layers of clothing**, plus gloves, socks, a warm hat and thermal underwear. Natural fibres such as wool are better than synthetic fabrics.
- **Take hot drinks regularly**, and eat regular meals.
- Use an **electric overblanket** which you can leave on all night to ensure that you are warm in bed.

Disabled people

People with disabilities have special requirements as far as safety is concerned. In particular, free and safe movement around the house and its surroundings is essential, and the ability to make use of its fixtures and services without unnecessary risk of danger or injury. This can be achieved through careful design of the home environment and sensible use of a variety of special equipment.

There is a wide range of advice and help available, both practical and financial, from local authorities and from a number of organisations and voluntary agencies. See Getting help on page 76 for more information.

Safe access to the home

For those with walking difficulties, being able to get into and out of the house easily is essential. Steps pose obvious problems, especially if the person concerned uses a walking-frame or wheelchair.

- Make sure that **steps** are in good condition, with a non-slip surface that drains freely so water or ice cannot make the surface slippery. Provide sturdy and easy-to-grip handrails at each side of the flight of steps, extending the rail by at least 300mm (12in) at each end of the flight for extra support. Make sure the steps are well lit at night, ideally by two-way switching that can be operated from either end of the flight.
- A gently sloping **ramp** to the front door is essential for wheelchair users, and is much safer than steps for anyone using a walking-frame. Concrete is preferable to a timber construction. The ramp should be 1.2m (4ft) wide and should have a slope of no more than 1 in 12; if space is available for a shallower ramp, a slope of 1 in 15 or even 1 in 20 will be easier to use. A kerb at least 100mm (4in) high along the open side of the ramp is essential to prevent a wheelchair running off the ramp; a **handrail** is also a must if the ramp will be used on foot. Lastly, there should be ample space at the top and bottom of the ramp for a wheelchair to manoeuvre.
- For people who walk with difficulty, a **four-wheeled shopping-trolley with a seat** and sturdy handle does double duty as a walking support.

Safe mobility within the home

Homes occupied by disabled people might need modifying in a variety of ways according to the type and degree of disability involved.

- Make sure that traffic routes are clear of obstructions. Rearranging or even removing some **furniture** can go a long way to making life easier.
- Most **doorways** are wide enough to allow only a standard wheelchair to pass through, so widening will probably be necessary for larger electric wheelchairs. Make sure that there is room for the door to open fully. It may be worth rehanging bathroom and WC doors to open outwards so there is more room to manoeuvre in the room itself.
- Make sure that **floorcoverings** are securely fixed in place. Carpets will wear along wheelchair traffic routes, so it may be worth considering a more durable floorcovering.
- Provide **grab-rails** on walls along traffic routes, and position **seats** to provide resting places *en route*.
- If you walk with difficulty or use a wheelchair and live in two-storey accommodation that cannot easily be reorganised for life on one level, consider installing a **stairlift** made to British Standard BS5776.

See also pages 71–3 for further advice.

Safety in the bathroom

The bathroom and WC can pose special safety problems for disabled people. Fortunately, there is a wide range of equipment available, including wall-mounted grab-rails, floor-mounted support frames, seats for use in the bath or in a shower cubicle, toilet height adjusters and non-slip mats.

General safety around the house

Being able to reach and operate things safely is important. Here are a few of the obvious possibilities; which of them are useful depends on your disability.

- Reposition **light switches and sockets** if necessary at more convenient levels. Fit appliances with plugs with easy-grip handles.
- Fit **taps** with lever handles. Some are replacement taps, others can be fitted to the existing tap handles. Many appliance controls can be similarly modified for ease of use.
- Modify **kitchen units and bedroom storage arrangements** to make things easier to reach, and to eliminate the risks involved in climbing on stools or chairs to reach high cupboards.
- Choose **special tools and equipment** to make life easier – to reach things, pick things up, grip them easily and so on. A wide range is available, especially for use in the kitchen.
- For people with **poor eyesight**, the home must be well lit and uncluttered. The use of distinctive colour contrast is also helpful, on fixtures and fittings and on edges at changes in level.
- If **poor hearing** is a problem, replace equipment giving an audible signal with equivalents giving a visual one. Door bells, alarm clocks and telephones are available with visual signals, or vibrator pads can be used as an alternative.

Getting help

Agencies and organisations that can provide help to disabled people include your social services department (social work department in Scotland, health and social services board in Northern Ireland), the Disabled Living Foundation*, disabled living centres (there are nearly 40 around the UK) and voluntary agencies such as Arthritis Care*, the British Red Cross*, and the Royal National Institutes for the Blind and for Deaf People.* RICA* publishes *Equipment for an easier life* and *Yellow Pages* lists equipment stockists and information agencies under the heading Disabled.

Accidents and emergencies

For disabled people living alone, being able to raise the alarm in the event of an accident or emergency is essential. The best solution is a community (or social) alarm system. You wear a small transmitter around the neck or wrist, or clipped to clothing, at all times, which when activated makes a telephone call to a relative, friend or 24-hour monitoring centre. This will bring help quickly. Ask for more details from RICA* or the Disabled Living Foundation*.

Pets

Household pets – especially dogs – and their paraphernalia are responsible for a surprising number of injuries in the home and garden, especially where there are children in the family. The accident statistics include the expected scratches and bites, people being tripped by playful pets, and injuries caused by hutches, cages, fish tanks and even pets' medication. We clearly share our homes with furry or feathered friends at our peril.

Safety with children

Many families keep pets for their children to play with, and it is this combination of children and play activity which leads to many accidents. Either the pet will accidentally scratch or bite the child during play, or will be provoked into attacking the child because it has been hurt or otherwise mishandled. A careful choice of pet, coupled with thorough education of the children by their parents, can go a long way towards reducing these accidents.

● **Choose pets** for your children sensibly. Before you buy, get as much advice as you can from bodies such as the Royal Society for the Prevention of Cruelty to Animals (RSPCA)★ and the People's Dispensary for Sick Animals (PDSA)★, both of which will supply you with leaflets giving information about choosing and looking after the more common pets. You can borrow books about pets from local libraries or buy them from pet shops and booksellers, and also get advice from pet shops and vets before choosing.

● Teach your children, especially the younger ones, **how to handle your pet** and what to avoid doing that could provoke a bite, scratch, peck or kick.

● Take special care with **babies or toddlers and pets**. Never leave a baby unattended in the company of family pets, either indoors or in the garden.

Safety in the house

The commonest cause of injury to both adults and children indoors, apart from scratches and bites, is someone falling over the pet – for example, when the animal moves unexpectedly or is lying unseen somewhere in the house. Pet equipment can cause injuries too.

- **Be alert**, especially on the stairs. Train dogs to sleep in a basket out of harm's way, and do not encourage pets into bedrooms; it is safest to keep them downstairs at all times. Close doors to restrict the movement of cats.
- Make sure that **kennels, hutches and cages** are safe to use, with no sharp edges or projections, especially if children look after the pets.
- Make sure that pet **feeding and grooming equipment** is kept out of the way when not in use.

Health and safety

Be aware of the potential problems of living with pets – everything from dealing with cat and dog fleas to the need for tetanus injections following a scratch or bite. Teach your children the importance of washing their hands after playing with or handling a pet, and of avoiding contact with pet's faecal matter.

Lastly, if you have to take a pet by car or public transport to the vet or to holiday accommodation, always use a proper carrying container so that it cannot escape or cause an accident.

CHAPTER 2

HOME SECURITY

A home security survey

In 1993 the police recorded over 700,000 burglaries. The British Crime Survey, carried out each year by the Home Office, asks people about crimes they have experienced, and whether or not these crimes were reported to the police. It estimates that another million homes were burgled, over and above the police statistics.

Whatever you may think of the merits of reporting a burglary to the police (only four per cent of the value of stolen goods are ever recovered), the facts are clear: your home stands a very real chance of being burgled this year, next year ... and for the foreseeable future. It is therefore up to you to tip the odds against the burglar. You can do this by making your property as secure as is compatible with a realistic lifestyle – no one should have to live in a fortress – and by thinking about security at all times. One lapse is all the burglar needs.

Finding the weak spots

Most burglars are opportunists, taking their chances if they spot a property that looks as if it offers quick and easy pickings. The ideal home is empty (80 per cent of burglaries take place when no one is at home), easy to break into, easy to get out of and not obviously overlooked. To see whether yours falls into this category, check its defences and look for its weak spots as if you were trying to get in without a key.

The front door
The front door may seem secure – it has a lock, after all. But what

A. Consider fitting a burglar alarm as a deterrent
B. Don't leave a window open where access would be easy from a flat roof
C. Install a time switch to certain lights in the house so that they will come on automatically even when you are out
D. Consider fitting external security lighting
E. Don't leave ladders lying about
F. Take stock of your fences and hedges – fences and walls should be secure and high, hedges thick

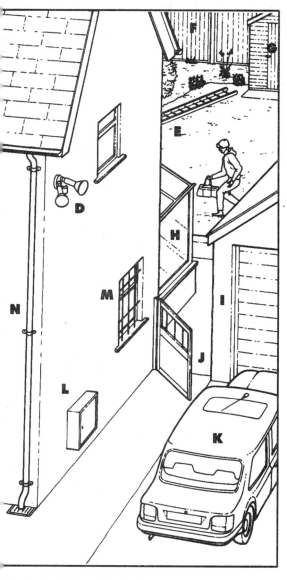

Sheds should be of the lock-up variety
Make sure that the conservatory is properly secured
Check up on garage locks
Keep the side gate closed to prevent easy access to the back of the house
Don't leave anything valuable in the car, remove the stereo system (if applicable) and use a crook lock

L. Demand to see an identity card from all callers unknown to you. Have external meter cupboards installed if you are out all day

M. Fit a metal grille over vulnerable windows

N. Paint drain-pipes with slippery anti-burglar paint

O. The panes of some double-glazed windows can easily be removed unless they are properly secured

P. Bikes, motorbikes and other vehicles are easy to steal if left lying around the front of the house

Q. Don't keep computers or other valuable equipment in view

R. Fit window locks

S. Cancel milk and newspapers when you go away

T. Never keep a spare key under the door mat or a flowerpot

U. Clear panels in the front door are less secure than solid ones

V. Fit a door viewer in a solid front door so that you can see who is at the door before opening it

W. Fit suitable door locks and a door chain/limiter

sort of lock is it? A surface-mounted lock relies for its security on the strength of its fixings, and it is easy for a burglar to see whether it is the only lock fitted to the door. He also knows that two or three well-aimed kicks may be all that is needed to burst the lock away from the door or its frame.

Glass panels in the door or in the door surround make life even easier unless the lock can be deadlocked; if it cannot, all the burglar has to do is break a pane and reach in to open the door.

Even a mortise lock may not be enough if the door is thin or the mortise has been cut over-large, weakening the door stile.

See pages 86 to 94 for advice on making your front door more secure.

Other doors

Back doors are generally even more vulnerable than front doors, for two reasons. They are by nature less secure, often incorporating areas of glass and usually being secured by a low-performance lock or just by surface-mounted bolts. They are also often concealed from view, allowing the burglar to force entry through them without being seen.

Outward-opening french doors and sliding patio doors have additional weaknesses. The hinge pins on the former can be removed, and the panes of the latter can be lifted out of their tracks unless anti-lift devices are incorporated in their design.

Clear access to the back of the house also makes life easier for the burglar if side gates are not bolted or if boundary fences are easy to climb.

See pages 86 to 94 for advice on making your back door and other doors more secure.

Windows

Windows left open, or held shut by simple catches that can be reached through open top lights or broken panes, provide the perfect entry and exit route for a burglar, especially if he can reach the window out of sight of prying eyes. Basement and semi-basement windows are especially attractive for this reason. Upstairs windows are also at risk if they can be reached from porch, extension or garage roofs, or if you leave ladders handy. Old cast-iron downpipes and soil pipes can also be scaled by an agile cat burglar, but he is unlikely to risk climbing their modern plastic counterparts because their light-duty fixings will not support his weight.

See pages 95 to 100 for advice on making your windows more secure.

Garages and conservatories

Integral or add-on garages with a door leading into the house are a classic security weak spot. The building may not itself be secure, and, once inside, the burglar can take his time to gain entry to the house without the risk of being seen. The same applies to conservatories and storm porches.

Detached garages and outbuildings also pose an indirect security risk, in that they often contain tools or other equipment that a burglar could use to force doors and windows.

See pages 100 to 103 for advice on making these buildings more secure.

The property as a whole

Mention has already been made of the risks of allowing easy access to the rear of your property, and the risk obviously increases after dark. If your fences or walls are easily climbed, broken down or missing altogether, a burglar could get over or through them. He can push through many hedges and other types of perimeter planting. If you have gates that are not bolted or locked, all he has to do is open them. And if you have high walls or hedges at the front of your property, these provide the perfect cover once he is on the property.

See pages 114 to 118 for advice on improving the security of your boundaries, and pages 118 to 121 for advice on security lighting.

Basic security precautions

Eighty per cent of burglaries happen when the house is empty. In many cases carelessness on the part of the householder is largely to blame; you may only have gone next door for a few minutes and left the door ajar, or popped out to the shops without locking the garage, but that is all the opportunity a burglar needs. And if you advertise the fact that the house is empty in the evening or when you go on holiday, you give him all the time in the world. You need to think security and be on your guard at all times.

Everyday security

The golden rule is to leave your house as secure as possible whenever you go out. This not only applies when you leave the property, however quickly you plan to return; it is also important if you and the family are in the back garden.

- **Close all windows** and make sure that catches and stays are properly engaged. Do not leave small top lights open; they may allow a burglar to reach a catch and let himself in, and a slim person could gain access via one. Shut windows at the front and side of the house when you are in the back garden.
- **Lock or bolt all doors** that open to the side or rear of the property, and remove keys from locks. Check doors that open into conservatories or integral garages, and also the exit doors from these buildings.
- **Bolt the side gate** and any other gates allowing access to the rear of your property.
- Make sure that **ladders** and other types of access equipment are out of sight or are chained up, and that separate garages or sheds containing tools or equipment of potential use to a burglar are secure.
- Try to keep **valuables out of sight** from the windows if you can. Handbags, wallets and small portable items such as cameras or portable stereos are always tempting if left on view. Draw the curtains in rooms containing the burglar's favourite consumer durables – televisions, video recorders, hi-fi systems and home computers.
- **Lock your front door**, and check that the lock has engaged. Double-lock it if the lock allows this. Do this from inside whenever you and the family are in the back garden.
- **Do not label your house keys** in case you lose them and they fall into the wrong hands. If you ever lose your keys, get the front door locks changed without delay; the cost of this may be covered by your house insurance policy.
- **Never leave a spare key** concealed anywhere near the front door; burglars know all the traditional hiding-places. If you are prone to locking yourself out or losing your keys, leave a spare set with two trustworthy neighbours (in case one is out when you

need it) but do not label it with your house name or number; if one of their houses is burgled and the key is found, your house could be next.

- **Draw the curtains** and leave some lights on and a radio playing if you are going out after dark.
- **Always identify callers** at your front door before you open it. Ask officials to produce identification, and check it carefully before allowing anyone in. Use a door chain or door viewer if you have one. Do not encourage young children to answer the door.

Going on holiday

Your house is particularly at risk when you go away on holiday. Apart from leaving it as secure as possible, there are   several other simple steps you should take to deter a would-be burglar.

- **Cancel the delivery of milk and newspapers.** If you receive local free newspapers, contact the distributor or leave a notice on the door requesting no deliveries. Do this a week or so before you depart so that you can check that it works.
- If your postman is in the habit of leaving **post projecting from your letter-box**, tackle him about it well before you go on holiday. Remove internal post cages in case they become crammed with post during your absence.
- Disconnect your **telephone answering machine**, or re-word your announcement to give the impression that you are only temporarily unable to answer.
- If possible, enlist the help of a **neighbour**, your Neighbourhood Watch coordinator (see pages 144–5) or nearby friend/relative to keep a regular eye on the property. He or she should at least keep the front door clear of unexpected deliveries, and, if you are prepared to leave a key, ask for curtains to be drawn and lights put on at night. If you are going to be away for a long period, ask for grass to be mown at the front of the property and leaves to be cleared. In winter, a few footprints in the snow will also make the house appear inhabited. (Some insurance policies for contents don't cover you if you are away for more than 30 days – see page 172.)
- Take **small valuables**, such as jewellery, away with you, or leave them with a friend or relative for safe keeping. Conceal larger

items from view if possible, and make a note of the serial numbers of things like televisions and video recorders in case the worst happens. Take identity photographs of antiques, paintings and other valuables. See pages 132–8 for more details about protecting your belongings.

● Set your **burglar alarm** if you have one, and enlist the help of a neighbour as keyholder in case the alarm goes off while you are away – either because of a break-in or by accident. Make sure he or she knows how to turn the alarm off and to re-arm the system. If it relies on a number combination, change this on your return for complete security.

● If you have no alarm, consider investing a few pounds in a **dummy alarm box**, available from most d-i-y superstores. It may well deter the opportunist thief.

Doors

Around 40 per cent of domestic burglaries involve entry through either the front or the back door. To make them more secure you need good locks properly fitted to a sound door and frame, plus some additional security devices selected to suit individual doors. Your front door is theoretically the most vulnerable because it is your final exit point from the building, so you cannot bolt or otherwise secure it from inside the house. However, other doors are at risk too, especially if they are out of sight or are within an integral garage or a conservatory where a burglar could work on them unnoticed. This section looks at how to make all your doors secure.

Locks for doors

Door locks can be surface-mounted or set into a slot (called a mortise) cut in the edge of the door. The former are quicker and easier to fit than the latter, but are generally less secure.

Surface-mounted locks
These are known as cylinder rim locks, and consist of three main components – the lock body, which is screwed to the inner face of the door, the cylinder, which passes through the door to its outer face, and the staple or keeper, which is screwed to the door frame.

The security of this type of lock depends largely on the strength of the fixings used to fit the lock and keeper in place; when fitting such a lock you may want to replace the fixings supplied with longer screws for extra security.

The simplest and cheapest type of rim lock is the nightlatch. This has a spring-loaded bolt operated by a key from outside the house and by an internal knob which you can lock with a movable button (for night-time security – hence the name). However, it is not secure from outside, since the bolt can be pushed back by inserting something flat and flexible between the door and its frame, and even if the knob is locked it could be unlocked by a burglar after breaking an adjacent pane of glass. He can also use a nightlatched door as a quick escape route after gaining access to the house somewhere else. To be secure, a rim lock must be capable of being deadlocked to prevent unauthorised forcing or operation without a key.

The way in which better rim locks provide this deadlocking feature varies. Some deadlock automatically when the door is closed, and the knob can be locked with a turn of the key – usually from either side, sometimes from the outside only. Others do not deadlock automatically, but can be deadlocked from either side using a key after the door has been closed.

The best security is provided by rim locks made to the requirements of British Standard 3621 for thief-resistant locks and carrying the BS Kitemark (the Kitemark is important in that it proves third party certification). Such a lock will incorporate features designed to resist attack by drilling into the lock, sawing through the bolt or forcing the mechanism. Many household insurance companies now insist that a lock made to this standard is fitted to your final exit door, and sometimes to other doors as well, before they will insure the property.

Most cylinder rim locks can be fitted to a door irrespective of whether it is hinged on the left or the right. Some models come in different versions for left-hand or right-hand doors, so check before you buy. There are also slim-line locks for glazed doors with narrow stiles.

How a cylinder lock works
The round casing that passes through the door contains a cylindrical plug into which the key fits. Both casing and plug contain a row of

holes, each containing a spring and a two-part pin. When locked, the holes are aligned internally and the springs push the pins into the holes in the plug to prevent it from turning inside the casing. When the key is inserted, the peaks and troughs in its edge push the pins up into the casing until the break between the two parts of each pin coincides exactly with the edge of the plug, allowing it to be turned to open the lock. The more pins such a lock has, the more secure it is.

Mortise locks

As their name implies, mortise locks fit into a slot or mortise cut in the edge of the door. They come in two varieties: one contains just a key-operated bolt, the other – known as a mortise sashlock – also contains a spring-operated latch. With both types, the bolt (and also the latch of a sashlock) engages in a keeper recessed into the door frame. The keeper may be an open plate or may have a boxed metal recess for extra resistance to forcing. Provided that the lock and keeper are carefully fitted, a mortise lock is likely to be stronger than a surface-mounted lock.

The simple mortise lock is used chiefly for securing front doors in conjunction with a cylinder rim lock; the former's lockable bolt provides a high degree of security at night or when the house is empty, while the rim lock provides medium security at all times and can be conveniently unlocked using its knob when the house is occupied.

The sashlock is used mainly for back doors, where the latch allows easy operation of the door for access to and from the garden and the lockable bolt provides good security at night or when the house is empty.

The lock mechanism is usually a lever type (see How a lever lock works, below), although some mortise locks are now available with a profile cylinder mechanism similar to that used in cylinder rim locks.

The security of a lever mortise lock depends on the number of levers it contains. Those with just two or three levers can be forced or picked relatively easily, and should be used only on internal doors. For external doors you need one with five, six or seven levers; the strongest types are, like the best cylinder rim locks, made to the requirements of BS3621 and carry the BS Kitemark.

A BS3621 lock has to have at least a thousand differs, or key

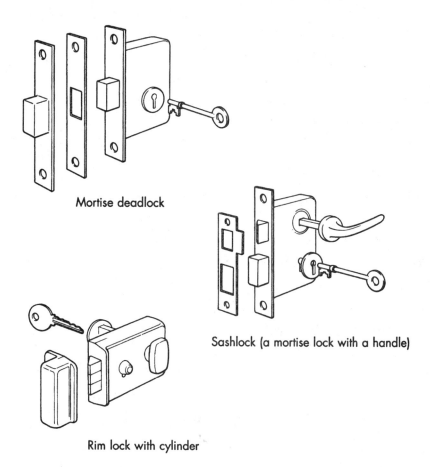

Mortise deadlock

Sashlock (a mortise lock with a handle)

Rim lock with cylinder

variations, so only one key in a thousand will open the lock – reasonable odds against a burglar having the same key as you. Five-lever locks offer up to 1,500 differs, while profile cylinder locks have several thousand unique key variations. In addition, the latter use the same type of key as a cylinder rim lock, and you can buy matching front- and back-door profile cylinder locks operated by the same key for convenience.

Mortise locks can be fitted to doors hinged at the left or right. Sashlocks are usually sold in mirror-image versions to suit the way the door opens, but those with a roller-style latch can be fitted to doors hinged at the left or right. As with cylinder rim locks, slim-line versions of both mortise locks and sashlocks are available for glass doors with narrow stiles.

How a lever lock works

The lock casing contains a number of plate-like levers, each with a central slot divided by two flanges and held down by a spring. As the key is turned in the lock, its flat portions – the wards – lift the various levers to align the slots so that the bolt knob can slide forward and push the bolt out. As the key is fully turned to its starting position, the levers fall back over the bolt knob and effectively deadlock it.

Locks for patio doors

Sliding patio doors are supplied with integral locks, and several different locking systems are used, ranging from a simple hook and bar to elaborate multi-point locking bolts. Old doors generally have a very low level of security, with the locks easy to force and the doors capable of being lifted off their tracks from outside. More modern doors are generally better, but unless they incorporate key-operated multi-point locking and anti-lift devices, you should add surface-mounted key-operated patio-door bolts to the door frame at top and bottom. These are now a requirement of many household insurance companies.

Take care when siting the bolt bodies so that the holes you have to drill in the doors will clear the edges of the double-glazed panes. Do not attempt to fit these bolts to uPVC patio doors, which should incorporate adequate built-in security features. Contact the door manufacturer for advice if you want to upgrade them further.

An alternative way of locking patio doors is with a locking bar. This fits between the frame against which the sliding door closes and the end of the fixed pane, locking the two together to prevent both forcing and lifting. It locks automatically on closing and is key-operated.

Bolts for doors

You can provide additional security for your doors by fitting bolts of various types. The simplest is the **surface-mounted barrel bolt**, which you can use to secure hinged back doors (including outward-opening french doors). However, these are only as secure as their screw fixings, and can be opened from outside if they can be reached through a broken pane in or beside the door, or through a letter-box or cat-flap in the door. Lockable key-operated types are better than ordinary bolts in this respect.

Mortise rack bolts are better for back doors. They have a cylindrical casing which fits in a hole drilled in the side or top edge of the door, and shoot a bolt into a hole drilled in the door frame at the turn of a key. For maximum security fit two to each door, one at the top and one at the bottom. The lock is operated from within the house only by a standard splined key, so a burglar could in theory operate it if he carried a matching key and was prepared to break a window or door pane to reach the lock. Keep your own rack bolt keys away from the door, stored somewhere handy in case you need to use the door as a fire escape.

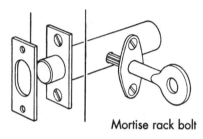

Mortise rack bolt

Hinge bolts (or dog bolts) are fixed steel pegs that are set into the hinged edge of the door and engage in holes drilled in the door frame when the door is closed. They prevent the hinged side of the door from being forced, and are a must for outward-opening french doors where the hinge pins are exposed and can be removed from outside. They are fitted in pairs, one just below the top hinge and the other just above the bottom hinge.

Extra security for doors

A high-security lock or other device is little use if the door itself is weak or the frame is in poor condition. An external door should be at least 45mm (1¾in) thick, and ideally of solid wood with no glass or thin plywood panels. If any of your doors are thinner than this, avoid using mortise locks unless you are prepared to reinforce the door (see below), and secure surface-mounted locks and bolts with the longest possible screws. For extra security:

- replace large panes of ordinary glass in doors and adjacent side panels with **wired or laminated glass** or polycarbonate sheeting
- consider having **metal security grilles** fitted to glass doors in vulnerable positions
- reinforce **large plywood door panels**, which can be kicked in for entry or escape, by screwing a panel of 12mm (½ in) thick plywood to the inner face of the door
- repair or replace **rotten door frames**.

Door reinforcing kits

You can buy metal plates which you fit to the inner and outer faces of the door that has been weakened by the installation of a mortise lock. The plates are fitted using security bolts so they cannot be removed from the outside. You can also fit frame reinforcing strips to the door frame to strengthen the locking points. Both plates and strips are available from locksmiths.

If the door frame moves when the door is slammed, its fixings need reinforcing. Secure each side of the frame to the walls by drilling through the wood with a twist drill, then on into the brickwork with a masonry drill. Insert a special long-sleeved plastic frame plug into the hole until its collar is flush with the frame and tighten the integral screw.

Door viewers

A door viewer is a two-part spyhole which fits in a hole drilled in a solid door, and is available in brass, chrome and bronze finishes to match other door furniture. One half of the viewer consists of a wide-angle lens housed in a slim tube which is inserted in the hole from the outside. The other half is inserted from the inside and is screwed into the lens section to lock the two parts together. You can tighten a knurled (ridged) type by hand, and a slotted type with a large screwdriver or the edge of a small coin. The inner part of the viewer may be fitted with a pivoting cover, which when closed will prevent an indoor light being visible from outside through the viewer.

When installing a door viewer, fit it at a height where it can be

DOOR SECURITY FITTINGS

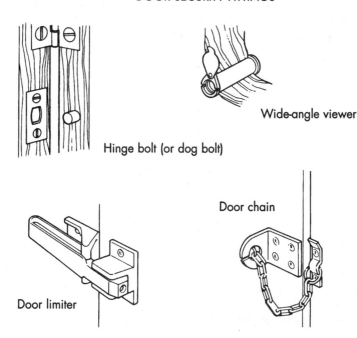

Wide-angle viewer

Hinge bolt (or dog bolt)

Door chain

Door limiter

used easily by all members of the family, and teach your children the importance of identifying callers before opening the door. Remember that you will not be able to use a door viewer at night unless your porch is well lit.

Door chains and limiters

A door chain or door limiter is a device that allows you to open the door a short way in order to vet callers while preventing someone from pushing his or her way in past you, and is essential if you have glazed doors where a door viewer would be pointless.

Two types of door limiter are available. The first holds the door ajar with a short length of strong chain, the second with a short rigid bar. In both cases the keeper is screwed to the inner face of the door, and the fitting with the chain or bar is secured to the door frame. The door has to be closed to allow the chain or bar to be released from the keeper, providing an extra degree of security since the caller cannot release it from outside. Whichever type is selected, its strength depends on the strength of the fixings, so it is vital to use the longest possible screws to attach the components to the door and its frame. Those supplied with many door limiters are simply not long enough to withstand an attempted forced entry.

Summary

Use this checklist to make sure that all your doors are secure and meet the requirements of household insurance companies.

- **Front door**: BS3621 mortise lock, cylinder rim lock (also ideally to BS3621), hinge bolts, door viewer (solid doors only), door chain or limiter (solid and glazed doors), security glazing in place of ordinary glass, door strengthening plates or reinforcing strips in vulnerable locations.
- **Hinged back doors**: BS3621 mortise sashlock (or BS3621 mortise lock and separate door latch), hinge bolts, mortise rack bolts, security glazing, door-strengthening measures in vulnerable locations.
- **Sliding patio doors**: key-operated surface-mounted locks at top and bottom, anti-lift device if not installed originally, door-locking bar.
- See pages 100 to 103 for advice on securing doors to **garages**, **sheds** and **conservatories**, and pages 103 to 105 for information on door **security grilles** and **shutters**.

Windows

Almost 60 per cent of burglaries involve entry through a window, most commonly one at the back of the house. In many cases the window was left open, or was forced because it had no secure locks. Few burglars will risk breaking large panes of glass unless they are confident that the noise will not alert suspicion, but small panes are more at risk if breaking one allows the burglar to reach a catch or stay and open the window. Window locks carefully chosen to suit the window types you have in your home will not prevent a determined burglar from gaining entry, but will deter the opportunist thief and will help to slow down even the professional house-breaker. This section looks at how to make your windows secure.

Locks for windows

A wide range of locking devices is available. They work in several different ways – securing a hinged casement or top light to its frame, locking sliding sashes together or preventing existing catches and stays from being released. Most are surface-mounted using screws and so are quick and easy to fit, although to install some types you have to drill a bolt hole and chisel out a recess for the bolt keeper plate. Mortise rack bolts and dual screws fit into holes drilled in the window, so take a little longer to install than surface-mounted types. All window locks are supplied complete with fixing screws, but many are woefully short. Since these locks often rely solely on the strength of the screw fixing for their strength, it makes sense to use the longest possible screws for all the fixings. It is also a good idea to fit two locks on casement windows more than about 1m (3ft 3in) high for extra security, especially downstairs; position one near the top and the other near the bottom of the casement.

When choosing locks for your windows, make sure that those you select are suitable for your window type and frame material; relatively few are suitable for metal windows, for example. If all your windows are a similar style, buy one lock and check that it can be fitted and operated correctly before buying the rest. The majority of window locks are available in white or brass; a few also come in dark brown to match stained woodwork.

Most of the locks on the market are operated by a standard key which a burglar might in theory also have about his person, but he will generally be loath to break glass to be able to operate the lock. Fit key-operated locks only if they give you extra peace of mind; the small number of key differs available does little to improve their security over locks operated with a standard key. Do not leave the keys in the locks, but keep them handy nearby both for everyday convenience and in case you need to open the window quickly in an emergency – as a fire escape, for example.

One or two locking devices allow the window to be locked in a slightly open position for ventilation – perhaps worth considering for sash windows or hinged top lights in ground-floor bedrooms, and for casement windows in children's bedrooms upstairs to prevent them from opening the window and falling out. However, you should not rely on these devices for high security when the house is empty; even if you are going out for just a short time, always lock windows shut tightly so that they cannot be forced.

Locks for casement windows

The commonest window locks for wooden casement windows fall into three main categories. The first type consists of two interlocking parts, one screwed to the casement and the other to the frame. The most satisfactory are those that lock automatically when the window is closed, since you cannot help but use them all the time. Others need a bolt to be pushed in or a bar swung into position to lock the window closed. All need a key, standard or cut, to release the lock.

The second type is fitted to the casement and shoots a bolt into a hole drilled in the frame to lock the window shut. The lock may be surface-mounted or set into a hole drilled in the edge of the casement – the mortise rack bolt. The former may be operated by pushing the bolt into place or by turning a knob; the latter requires a standard splined key to wind the bolt in and out.

The third type prevents the casement stay or the window latch (called a cockspur handle) from being moved. If your casement stays have holes, you can use the locking pin type; this replaces the casement stay pin and can be fitted with a key-operated locking nut – inexpensive and easy to install, so ideal for hinged top lights. For stays without holes, use a stay bolt which has a key-operated bolt to hold the stay down. To secure the window latch, you can replace it with a lockable latch or fit a key-operated bolt that prevents the handle from being moved.

Most of these locks can be used on top-hung, centre-mounted or bottom-hung wooden pivot windows. A few – notably the window stay clamp and latch bolt – can also be fitted to some types of metal windows; check carefully that the locks you choose suit your windows before buying in bulk.

Locks for sash windows

Most locks for sash windows work by preventing the sashes from sliding past each other. The simplest to fit is a two-part surface-mounted device that is installed on top of the meeting rails; the two parts are locked together with a key or a push-in bolt when the window is closed. You need a key to open either type.

A variation on this type is a one-part lock that is mounted on the top rail of the inner sash, close to the side of the window, and shoots a bolt into a hole drilled in the side of the upper sash. With this type, you can drill further holes higher up the sides of the top sash to allow the window to be locked in a slightly open position for ventilation. Again, a key is needed to release the bolt.

The alternative to surface-mounted bolts for sash windows is the dual screw. This consists of a threaded bolt which engages in a matching internally threaded sleeve inserted through a hole drilled in the top rail of the inner sash. A plain metal sleeve is inserted in a stopped hole drilled in the bottom rail of the outer sash, and when the bolt is screwed fully home with its key it securely locks the two sashes together. With some types, a simple hole is drilled in the outer sash, and a small keeper plate is fitted over it. You can leave the upper sash locked open for ventilation if the screws are fitted close to the sash sides and additional sleeves are inserted in the side rails of the top sash. You need to take considerable care to get the two threaded sleeves accurately aligned when installing dual screws, or you may have difficulty in screwing in the bolt.

All these locking devices are best used in pairs for maximum security. Dual screws and some push-bolt types can be cut with a saw blade inserted from outside between the sash rails, but cutting through the bolts would take a burglar several minutes.

Locks for problem windows

French windows, or french doors as many people call them, open outwards like a casement window, and are best secured with a mortise rack bolt or strong surface-mounted bolt fitted at the top and bottom of each casement so that the bolt passes into a hole in the head and sill of the door frame. Add a mortise sashlock to the meeting rails.

The butt hinges used to hang french windows are a security risk because they are exposed outside the frame. This means that a burglar can punch out the hinge pins and lift out the doors. Guard against this by fitting two hinge bolts to the closing edge of each door.

Louvred windows, especially older types, are a serious security risk because the glass slats can be lifted out of their holders. If you have a window of this type, use an epoxy resin adhesive to secure the slats in their mounts. Replace the window with fixed glass or an opening casement if it is in a vulnerable position.

Windows with traditional leaded lights are also a security risk because it is fairly easy for a burglar to prise up the soft lead cames holding the panes in place so that one can be removed for access to a window catch. You can improve the security of such windows to some extent by fitting a window latch bolt, but in vulnerable locations a security grille on the inside of the frame is the only effective way of preventing entry.

Plastic (uPVC) windows come with built-in locks – usually highly secure multi-point bolts on the latest models. However, some earlier types of these windows had relatively poor locks, and it is not easy to find add-on locks suitable for fitting to their reinforced plastic framing members. If you have such windows and want to improve their security, contact the original supplier or window manufacturer for advice, or a locksmith (see the Master Locksmiths Association*) if the supplier or manufacturer is unknown or no longer trading.

Double-glazed windows with sealed units held in place by externally fitted gaskets are an unexpected security risk, because with some frame types it is possible to remove the gaskets and simply lift the sealed unit out of its frame. If you have such windows, contact the supplier or manufacturer for advice on making the gaskets secure. If you are choosing new windows, check that their gaskets are fitted internally.

Extra security for windows

As with doors, there is little point in fitting good locks to your windows if the fixings are inadequate or if, in the case of wooden windows, the wood is rotten. For extra security:

- repair or replace **any rotten sections** of casement and sash windows and their frames
- use the **longest possible fixing screws** to secure surface-mounted locks and other components to wooden windows. Use self-tapping screws to secure locks to metal windows
- if fitting **mortise rack bolts**, check the lock diameter against the thickness of the casement first to make sure you will not be weakening the wood unduly. The hole for the lock body should be no more than half the thickness of the casement
- consider fitting fixed or lockable **security grilles** to protect

windows in vulnerable locations – in basements and semi-basements, for example. See pages 103 to 105 for more details.

Safety in the event of fire

When you are fitting window locks, remember that you may need to use an upstairs window as an escape route or rescue point in the event of fire.

● Hang the **key** for any window likely to be used as an escape route on a hook close to the window where it is invisible from outside but can be easily reached in an emergency, and make sure everyone in the family knows where the key is.

● If you are worried about finding keys in a hurry, fit window locks that all use the **same standard key,** so any key will open all the windows.

● If you have an **upstairs window at the front of the house** that is completely inaccessible without a ladder, designate that as your final rescue point and do not fit a lock to it.

● Make sure you have one or more **smoke detectors** in the house. They will give you valuable extra minutes to escape if a fire starts. See pages 52–3 for more details about choosing and installing them.

Summary

Use this checklist to make sure that all your windows are secure and meet the requirements of household insurance companies.

● **Casement** and **pivot windows**: any key-operated locking device. Fit two on windows more than 1m (3ft 3in) high.

● **Sash windows**: two surface-mounted locks or bolts, or two dual screws.

● **French windows**: mortise rack bolts at the top and bottom of each casement, a mortise sashlock on the meeting rails and two hinge bolts per casement.

● **Windows with leaded lights**: key-operated latch bolt, security grille in vulnerable locations.

● **uPVC windows**: contact the supplier, the manufacturer or a locksmith if yours need improved security.

- See below for advice on securing windows in **conservatories**, **garages** and **outbuildings**, and pages 103 to 105 for information on **window grilles** and **shutters**.

Conservatories, garages and outbuildings

Conservatories have become one of the top-selling home improvements of recent years. However, because most conservatories usually have access from the house – or at least enclose one or more room windows – they pose a new security risk. If the conservatory itself is not secure, a burglar can gain entry to it and can then work unseen on a door or window within it to gain access to the house. The same risk applies to integral garages with a door leading directly into the house; if the garage is not secure, the burglar can then take his time breaking into the house itself.

Garages, whether attached or detached, need to be secure for another very good reason: they often contain ladders and tools which a burglar could use to gain entry to the house. So do garden sheds. And it is surprising how many people leave ladders and tools lying about in the open in their back garden. A ladder is a gift to any burglar, and even a humble garden spade makes a very good lever for forcing doors and windows. Tidy up and lock up is the rule.

Conservatories

If you are buying a new conservatory, pay particular attention to its security provisions, especially if it is made from uPVC rather than timber. Doors from conservatory to garden should have multi-point key-operated locks; in addition, outward-opening hinged doors should also have hinge bolts, and sliding patio doors should incorporate an anti-lift device. All the windows should have key-operated locks, and all the glazing should be in toughened glass that is Kitemarked and marked 'made to British Standard BS6206 Class A'. Conservatories with plastic roofs offer potentially easy access – all the more reason to ensure that the door between the conservatory and the house is secure.

If you have an existing conservatory, subject it to an intensive security inspection. See pages 86 to 92 for ways of improving the security of both the doors leading into the garden and those connecting the conservatory to the house, and pages 94–9 for ways of securing the conservatory windows. If the glass is not toughened, consider having special security glazing film fitted to it for both security and safety reasons; see the previous page for more details.

If you have a burglar alarm system (see pages 105 to 113 for more details), have it extended to protect the conservatory too – either with an extra door sensor on the door leading to the garden, or with an additional movement sensor (see page 120) within the conservatory itself.

Garages

Depending on its design, your garage may offer a burglar up to four points of entry – the main door, a side door or a window, and through an integral garage ceiling. If the garage is integral or attached to the house and you have a burglar alarm system, it is well worth having the system extended to cover the garage as well.

Side-hung doors
Old outward-opening side-hung doors pose a particular problem since, like your front door, they have to be locked from outside. Worse still, they have external hinges and a thief may be able to knock out a hinge pin to gain access. If they contain small panes of glass, breaking one for access to an old-fashioned nightlatch or a simple barrel bolt on the inside will also prove no problem. Tackle each weak spot separately:

- Fit two **hinge bolts** to the hinged edge of each door.
- Fit **lockable surface-mounted bolts** to the top and bottom of the door that closes first, and drill holes in the head of the frame and the garage floor to accept the projecting bolts. These will hold this door firmly closed and ensure that the main lock (see below) on the other door will be secure.
- Fit a **five-lever mortise lock** to the meeting edge of the doors, and add reinforcing plates over the outside of the lock position. Alternatively, fit a stout hasp, staple and high-security padlock. Attach the hardware with small bolts and nuts rather than screws so it cannot be levered out of the woodwork.

Up-and-over doors

Modern up-and-over doors are not much more secure than hinged types unless they are operated by an electric door opener. Very few existing garage doors have high-security locks, and, once picked, the door can be opened easily. Follow these guidelines:

- Contact the **door manufacturer** – usually identified on the door's inner face – or a locksmith (see Master Locksmiths Association*) for advice about fitting a more secure lock to the door.
- Fit a special **garage door mortise rack bolt** to each bottom corner of the door.
- Fit a **floor-mounted ground lock** – this locks the bottom edge of the door to the garage floor slab in the same way as locks secure pull-down shop shutters.
- For garages with a side door, or those with direct access to the house – when going away on holiday, attach a **G-cramp** to the door track inside the garage just behind each door roller. This will prevent the door from being opened from outside even if the lock is forced.

Personal (side) doors

How you improve the security of a personal (side) door depends on its type. If it is a ledged-and-braced door, fit lockable surface-mounted bolts horizontally to the top and bottom ledges at both the hinged and opening edges of the door. If it is a flush door, fit a five-lever mortise sashlock and add two surface-mounted bolts and a pair of hinge bolts.

Garage windows

If your garage has windows and you need to open them for ventilation when working in the garage, any type of window lock will improve their security. See pages 95–8 for more details of the various types available. If you do not need the windows to open, simply screw them shut from outside and grind away the screw slots or recesses so they cannot be undone. To prevent anyone climbing in through a broken pane, screw a piece of wood or metal securely across the opening to reduce the size of the gaps.

Garden sheds

Most people keep tools in a garden shed which could be of use to a burglar, and few are at all secure. Sheds without windows are best, since no one can see what is inside.

- If yours has **windows** and you do not need to open them for ventilation, screw them shut and grind away the screw slots or recesses, as described for garage windows above. Otherwise fit window locks.
- Consider replacing thin window glass with **plastic sheeting**, or at least stick clear self-adhesive plastic film over the inside so it will not break easily.
- Secure the **shed door** with a stout hasp and staple and a high-security padlock, as described for side-hung garage doors above.
- Consider buying a **shed/garage alarm system**.
- Use clutch-head screws to secure **external hinges** to prevent them being undone for access.

Grilles and shutters

Some homes have windows – notably in basements and semi-basements – that are extremely vulnerable to attack by burglars because they are usually hidden from view. A determined burglar will defeat any window lock given time, and will be less worried about breaking glass to gain entry when no one can see or hear where the noise has come from. The only foolproof security for such vulnerable windows is a security grille or shutter.

Types of grille

You can choose one of four types of security grille. The first is a **fixed steel or wrought-iron screen**, which is permanently mortared into the window reveal outside the window frame, or screwed into the brickwork with security screws. Its drawbacks are that it may look unsightly from outside the house (although decorative grilles are available), may cut down light within it, and will of course prevent the window from being used as a fire exit. Such grilles are made to measure by security hardware suppliers and some decorative metal gate manufacturers (and also by local blacksmiths, if you can find one).

The second type is a **removable grille** which is fitted inside the window reveal and secured by locks – and ideally a quick-release mechanism for use in the event of an emergency. Both fixed-frame and telescopic types are available. Hinged types can also be fitted outside entrance doors for extra security. Telescopic types, which expand to fit the window reveal and are then locked in place, have the advantage that you can remove them easily when you are at home and fit them only when you leave the house.

The third type is a **fixed screen**, which is simply screwed to the inside of the window reveal or to the framing around a glazed panel in a door. This type is the least expensive, and diamond lattice types that resemble leaded lights when installed are not unpleasant to look at either. Do not use them at any windows likely to be used as fire escape routes, however.

The last type is also by far the most expensive: a **sliding concertina barrier** resembling old-fashioned lift doors, which is mounted on tracks within the window (or door) opening. The gates can be pushed back and concealed behind the curtains when the house is occupied, and drawn across and locked when it is empty. This type of grille is particularly suitable for protecting french doors, especially those in semi-basements where you need a combination of everyday access and excellent security.

Fitting grilles

As long as you have measured up your window or door carefully before placing your order, installing any type of grille is well within the capability of the average do-it-yourselfer used to making firm fixings in wood or masonry. Use the longest possible screws at all times for maximum resistance to forcing.

If ordering a fixed external grille, specify the positions of the fixing lugs accurately to ensure that they will coincide with the mortar courses in the brickwork. For sliding concertina gates, check whether the top track can be fixed to the wall above the door reveal rather than to the underside of the opening; with the former, the fixings will be easier to make, and it is also simpler to get the top track truly level even if the lintel is slightly out of true.

If you are fitting a removable grille, make sure that all members of the family know how to release it in case of an emergency.

Security shutters

The ultimate security barrier for doors and windows is an aluminium security shutter. However, this is also the most expensive option and is worth considering only if you live in a very high-risk area and want complete security both at night and whenever the building is unoccupied. Each shutter is tailor-made to suit the opening concerned. You will need to find out from your local authority if planning permission is required.

Security shutters resemble a roller blind in operation. When raised, they are housed in a box at the top of the window or door opening, and when closed their edges run in enclosed tracks shaped to resist forcing at each side. They can be raised or lowered manually or by an electric motor from within the house, and lock automatically on closing.

Anti-burglar paint

If you have windows that could be accessible to an agile burglar prepared to climb a cast-iron soil pipe or drain pipe on your house walls, there is one final step you can take to protect them: apply anti-burglar paint to the pipes. This is a special non-drying coating that makes the pipes almost impossible to climb (and leaves the burglar with extremely dirty hands). It is available in black only, and should be applied to all external pipes of this sort from a height of about 1.8m (6ft) above the ground to avoid the risk of accidental contact by family and pets.

D-i-y alarm systems

If you have followed the advice given in the preceding pages, your home will be as secure against burglary as it realistically can be. There is just one more step that you can take if your budget allows: fit a burglar alarm.

Your reasons for doing this will vary. Some people want one because they believe it will help to deter burglars, and there is some evidence that opportunist thieves will steer clear of a visible alarm box for fear of drawing attention to themselves if an alarm sounds. Some want an alarm because they have already been burgled and will do anything to stop it happening again. A misguided few want one because they believe it will help catch criminals red-handed by summoning a horde of vigilante neighbours and a fast-response police force to the scene before the miscreant can escape. However, this is a somewhat forlorn hope, since most people nowadays studiously ignore any sounding alarm (they are more likely to complain about the noise nuisance) and the police admit that investigating domestic burglary is a low priority. Lastly, more and more people are installing them to get a significant reduction in their household insurance costs, which suggests that the insurance companies at least think that alarms have some beneficial effect on the crime statistics and the resulting level of insurance claims they can expect.

Whatever your reason for wanting an alarm, you have a straight-forward choice to make between fitting your own system or calling in a professional firm to do the job for you. This section looks at d-i-y alarm kits; see pages 109 to 113 for information on professionally installed systems.

A choice of systems

There are three options available to you if you decide to install your own alarm. The first, and currently the most popular due to its ease of installation, is the so-called wireless system. The second is the traditional fully wired type, less expensive to buy but more time-consuming to fit in the home. The third is the dummy alarm box, a metal or plastic casing which you fit to your house wall to convince burglars that you actually have an alarm system. This last type costs only a few pounds and is well worth considering because of its modest deterrent effect if you cannot afford to consider having a proper alarm system (but see also Alarms for outbuildings below).

There are two British Standards for d-i-y alarm systems: BS6707 (Specification for intruder alarm systems for consumer installation) and BS6799 (Code of Practice for wire-free intruder alarm systems).

Wireless systems
With a wireless alarm system, the various movement detectors and door/window contacts transmit signals to the control panel using

radio waves, which greatly speeds up the installation; a typical system will take some three or four hours to fit. However, with most there is still some wiring to do – linking the external alarm to the control panel, for example, and providing a mains power supply. You can simply plug or wire the alarm into a power circuit, but if your house has a residual current device (RCD) protecting its power-circuit wiring, you should take the alarm's power supply from its own five-amp fuseway in the consumer unit to avoid the slight chance of a tripped-off RCD cutting off the supply and draining the alarm batteries.

The main components of a typical system are:

- the **main control panel** (which usually has a back-up battery)
- an **internal sounder**
- an **external bell**, often incorporating a flashing strobe light and in some cases a back-up battery
- **interior movement detectors**
- **door/window contacts**
- **panic button(s)**, which allow you to set off the alarm immediately, even if the system is not itself armed, if an intruder barges past as you open the front door, or if you hear suspicious noises downstairs during the night. Most panic buttons are shielded to prevent their accidental operation, and need a key to switch them off once they have been activated.

Most wireless alarm kits actually contain only the bare essentials – enough to protect a flat or very small house. You have to pay extra for additional movement detectors and door/window contacts (most kits provide just one of each) and this can add substantially to the overall cost. However, this type of system does have one big advantage over wired systems: you can take it with you when you move house. You may also be able to use it to protect garages and garden sheds.

Other features to check when choosing a system include the number of separate control zones it offers (to enable you, for instance, to move around upstairs while the ground floor is alarmed), how long a period you have to leave the house after setting the alarm and how quickly you have to deactivate it on your return. Look too for the presence of features designed to prevent tampering (with the external bell, for example), to cut off the external bell after a pre-set time and to re-set the system automatically after the alarm has sounded. Most systems have a beeper to remind you that the alarm is on when you come home.

In addition to the main kit components listed above, most manufacturers offer additional options. These include glass break detectors, remote-control units, autodiallers (these call a pre-set telephone number if the alarm is triggered) and smoke detectors. You should have this last option in your home anyway, but if you are away from home a lot there is some merit in having detectors that will sound an external alarm; if a fire breaks out it will alert a forewarned neighbour who can then call the fire brigade and save your house from severe damage or destruction.

The most difficult part of fitting a wireless alarm is ensuring that the movement detectors cover as much as possible of the room in which they are installed. Set them in position and test their efficiency with just the internal sounder connected to avoid unduly annoying your neighbours. When siting detectors, try to avoid obvious obstructions to their viewing angle. Do not use them in rooms containing a real fire unless you can screen it from view when you go out; moving flames can trigger the detector. Test the system at least once a year by simulating a break-in and checking the operation of movement detectors.

If you install a wireless system and live near public services that use radio communication systems – a police, fire or ambulance station or an airport, for example – check with the kit manufacturer about the possibility of radio frequency interference.

Lastly, remember to tell your local authority's environmental health department that you have installed an alarm, so they know whom to contact in the event of a real or false alarm. If possible, appoint a trusted neighbour or a nearby friend or relative as key-holder. Make sure the keyholder knows how to deactivate the alarm and, if necessary, how to reset it.

Wired systems

Wired alarm systems consist of broadly the same components and offer many of the same features as wireless ones, with the obvious difference that everything is linked by slim wires instead of radio waves, so they cost less. One big point in their favour is that any additional components you want to add to expand the system are also much cheaper to buy than their wireless equivalents. However, the installation can be very time-consuming – especially if you want to conceal the wiring everywhere – although it is not difficult so long as you follow the instructions carefully. Allow around a full working day for installation – more if you want contacts on all your windows and doors.

As with wireless alarm systems, you should inform the environmental health department of your local authority when you install a wired alarm system, and appoint someone to act as keyholder if you are unavailable in the event of a real or false alarm. Test the system at least annually.

Alarms for outbuildings

If you store tools, ladders and the like in a garage or outbuilding, you should of course take steps to make the buildings as secure as you can – see pages 101 to 103. However, protecting them with their own burglar alarm will certainly give you both peace of mind and also an early warning that an intruder is about. Unless you have a wireless alarm system that can be extended to cover outbuildings, you will need a separate alarm.

Several manufacturers now offer small battery-powered alarms which can be attached to garage and shed doors, and which emit a piercing sound when triggered. Some are key-operated; others are operated by entering a code on a key-pad.

You could in theory also use one or more of these door alarms as a rudimentary alarm system for your home. The sound of the alarm will act as a valuable burglar deterrent if you are out, and will give extra night-time security when everyone is asleep.

Professional alarm systems

If you want a burglar alarm system but do not feel up to installing it yourself, there are plenty of professional firms waiting to help – at a price. You will have to turn to them anyway if you want a monitored system – one connected to a monitoring station that alerts the police if a break-in occurs – rather than a simple bell-only alarm. If you decide to follow this route, you need to know at the outset about the choices available to you.

Choosing an installer

If you open your *Yellow Pages* telephone directory at the Burglar Alarms & Security Equipment section you will be confronted with literally dozens of local firms, and also a few companies operating nationwide.

Anyone can set up a security company in this country, but there are three bodies in the security industry (see below) which set standards and controls for their member firms, so it makes sense to pick a member of one of them to carry out your installation. The only safe way to find a competent installer who does not belong to one of these three organisations is through personal recommendation.

Whoever you employ should state that the installation and maintenance of the alarm systems they sell conform to the British Standard for intruder alarms in buildings (BS4737).

National Approval Council for Security Systems★
Generally referred to as NACOSS, this is an independent regulatory body with about 500 registered members. All have to conform to the installation standards of BS4737 and must follow detailed codes of practice. Its inspectors monitor registered firms and their installations at regular intervals. Most household insurance companies insist on an alarm installed by a NACOSS member before they will grant a discount on their policy premium.

British Security Industry Association★
The BSIA covers many areas of the security industry. Member firms must conform to British Standards requirements and to the BSIA's code of practice, and those installing alarms will always also be NACOSS members.

Security Systems and Alarms Inspection Board★
The SSAIB inspects its 250 enrolled installers' work on a random basis and deals with complaints (if any).

You can also get details of local alarm installers with a proven track record from the police; contact your local Crime Prevention Officer for advice.

Ask at least three companies to visit your home, explain their recommendations and give you a detailed quotation of the likely cost. Knowing what is on offer before they arrive will ensure that you ask the right questions.

Choosing the system

The first choice you have to make is whether to have a stand-alone alarm or one linked to a monitoring station. The latter will generally cost more, but gives you the additional peace of mind of knowing that someone will call the police if the system detects a break-in at any time of the day or night. Most such systems also offer fire protection, and some feature a personal emergency pager – worth considering if you live alone and are frail, disabled or in poor health.

The second choice is the system itself, and here you are in the hands of the salesperson who visits your home. He or she should ask you about how you use your home, should identify any weak points that need additional protection, and should thoroughly explain the system on offer and its components. You are most likely to be offered a fully wired system, although some firms install wireless systems too. Specific points to ask about include the following.

- **Zones**. The system should allow you to protect separate zones of the house individually, especially the downstairs at night and rooms where pets sleep (most systems can be set *not* to react to small creatures). It is useful to have spare zone capacity in case you want to expand the system in the future.
- **Personal attack** and **fire protection**. The system should include panic buttons by the front door and in the master bedroom so that you can trigger the alarm even if it is not set. A monitored system offering fire protection is connected to a series of smoke detectors.
- **Tamper circuits**. The system should be designed to detect attempts at cutting off any of the detection zones or the wires to the external bell-box. The more separate circuits it has, the easier it is to find where the tampering has occurred.
- **Walk-test facility**. This allows you to check the operation of the detection devices without triggering the external alarm.
- **Code numbers**. Modern alarms have a numeric key-pad and are set and disarmed by entering a four-digit code which you can

select and change at will. Some offer the option of having two or more different codes, allowing one to be used as a temporary code – by a neighbour minding the house while you are on holiday, for example. Some control panels have a separate key-pad, allowing you to position the main control panel out of sight – in a cupboard, say.

- **Power supply**. Ask how the system will be powered, and how much any necessary mains wiring work will cost. The ideal is for the system to have its own circuit, which should *not* be protected by a residual current device (RCD) in case an electrical fault elsewhere in the house cuts its power supply and its back-up battery runs down.
- **Phone code changes**. In view of the fact that UK national dialling codes may change from time to time, ask what is involved in any necessary reprogramming of a monitored alarm system and who has to pay for the work.

Maintenance

Alarm companies generally encourage you to sign a service or maintenance contract with them, and such a contract is mandatory with monitored alarms to cover the cost of the monitoring service. The police and BS4737 both recommend regular servicing, since around 90 per cent of alarms are falsely activated. However, it pays to examine the cost and the length of such a contract; the company can put the fees up as and when it likes, unless the contract states otherwise, and fees are often payable in advance. ·

If you have a bell-only alarm, you are not obliged to take out a contract with the firm installing it (unless your house insurance company insists). The ideal is to have a one-year contract, renewable annually, which you can review on your terms. Whatever service contract you take on, check what will be covered in terms of parts, labour and call-out charges, especially outside normal working hours.

Rent or buy?

Most firms offer a choice of outright purchase of the equipment or a rental agreement where you buy the circuit wiring but rent the other system components. Purchasing outright is generally the more expensive option, but does avoid the risk of tying yourself to difficult contractual obligations. A rental agreement allows the firm to increase prices at will, often obliges you to agree to a lengthy maintenance contract and gives the firm the right to remove its equipment if a dispute arises over costs or service levels.

Summary

If you are buying a professionally installed burglar alarm system, follow these guidelines to ensure that you get the installation you want at a price you can afford.

- Check whether your **household insurance** company offers a discount if you have an alarm, and find out whether it insists on installation and/or maintenance by a NACOSS member. Remember that if you have the alarm installed and claim a discount on your insurance premium, you may not be fully covered if you fail to set it and a burglary occurs.

- Invite **quotations** from at least three firms. Include any that are recommended by neighbours or friends.

- Decide in advance whether you want a **bell-only or a monitored alarm**. The latter generally costs a little more to install and a lot more in service costs.

- When the salesperson arrives, ask to see some form of identification. Explain **what kind of alarm** you want, outline which areas of the house you want protected as separate zones and state how much money you are prepared to spend. Check that the alarm and its installation will conform to BS4737. Don't allow yourself to be sold an over-complex system; the simpler it is (within reason), the more likely you are to use it and the less likely you are to be plagued with self-induced false alarms.

- Insist on **outright purchase** unless you have good reasons for preferring a rental agreement.

- Check the terms of **service contracts** meticulously. Avoid signing lengthy contracts, especially those requiring advance payments, and research service options with other local firms.

- Make sure you get a **detailed quotation** in writing from each firm.

Boundaries

Protecting your house from burglars is obviously your primary concern. However, you do not really want them on your property at all, especially at the back of the house, and the best way of preventing this unauthorised access is to make sure you have secure boundaries. This is especially important if your property adjoins a road, a footpath, a railway line or a public space – a recreation ground, for instance.

Back garden security

To deter anyone trying to get into your back garden from an adjacent property or area, you need two-metre high perimeter walls or fences. These should be sturdy and difficult to climb. Impenetrable thorny plants grown up trellises can also do the trick; only the very thick-skinned will try to climb through a closely planted pyracantha hedge, for example.

Secure boundaries are also important if you have children or pets, since neither will be able to escape unnoticed.

Garden walls

A masonry garden wall should be a minimum of 1.8m (6ft) high; you can build one to a height of 2m (6ft 6in) without the need for planning permission unless the boundary adjoins a highway, when consent is needed for a wall over 1m (3ft 3in) high. Consent (and professional advice) must be sought if you intend building perimeter walls higher than 2m (6ft 6in).

The wall should be at least 225mm (9in) thick and should have reinforcing piers 450mm (18in) square every 3m (10ft) for strength. A straight run more than 6m (20ft) long should also include flexible vertical joints running from top to bottom to accommodate any slight movement in the wall structure. To make climbing difficult, joints in the outer face of the wall should be flush-pointed and the top of the wall should be finished with a tiled ridge. Broken glass set in mortar is not recommended, but if you want to prevent unauthorised access a row of steel spikes is an effective deterrent.

Fences

As with walls, you can erect fences up to 2m (6ft 6in) high around your back garden without planning permission unless it adjoins a highway, when consent is needed for fences over 1m (3ft 3in) high. The most secure type of fencing is a post-and-rail type clad on the outer face with overlapping vertical boards, since this is both strong (so long as it is in good condition) and difficult to climb. Top it with trellis 600mm (2ft) high to deter climbers further; growing plants up this will also improve your privacy without infringing the planning rules.

Panel fences are less secure for several reasons. Most are only 1.8m (6ft) high, their horizontal components provide useful footholds, and they are generally relatively flimsy.

Avoid ranch-style fencing with horizontal boards, even if these are closely spaced; they are as simple as a ladder to climb over.

Gates

If you have a gate in your back garden, pay attention to its security too. If the gate leads to the front of the house, fit barrel bolts to its garden side low enough to prevent anyone reaching over the gate and undoing them. If it leads to a rear access or public property, lock it; use a stout hasp and staple on a wooden gate and a chain on an ornamental metal one, both secured by a sturdy padlock, and keep it locked except for when you need to use it.

Defensive planting

If you hate walls and fences, you can still protect your property by planting burglar-deterrent species along the perimeter. This will take time, of course, but you can provide security in the meantime with a wire mesh fence 2m (6ft 6in) high which will be hidden once the shrubs have matured and which will provide a secondary line of defence. The following species all have thorns or prickly leaves that will deter even the hardiest intruder:

- *Berberis sargentiana*: an evergreen, grows to 2m (6ft 6in), with stout spines up to 30mm (1¼ in) long
- *Berberis wilsoniae*: grows to only 1m (3ft 3in), but spreads well to form a dense, thorny mound
- *Chaenomeles cathayensis*: has formidable but attractive spines, white flowers and decorative fruit
- *Crataegus crus-galli*: a small tree with viciously thorny branches, white flowers followed by red haws and red autumn foliage

- *Hippophaë rhamnoides*: a shrub with huge spines (and orange-yellow berries if both sexes are interplanted)
- *Ilex aquifolium ferox*: one of many hollies that make attractively impenetrable evergreen hedges (with berries on female plants if both sexes are interplanted); slow-growing but will reach a height of 6m (20ft)
- *Pyracantha*: most varieties will produce a viciously prickly hedge up to 4m (13ft) high.

General back garden security

Despite your best efforts, a would-be burglar might still gain access to your back garden. If he does, do not make it easy for him to steal things or to use garden or d-i-y equipment to break into the house.

- Make sure that **outbuildings** are securely locked up (see page 103 for more details). Tools stored there could be used to gain entry to the house, and valuable powered gardening equipment could simply disappear.
- If you have to store a **ladder** in the garden, hang it on stout brackets attached to a wall or fence and secure it to them with a padlocked chain so it cannot be used for access.
- Be aware that burglars have been known to use **garden furniture or ornaments** to smash rear windows, especially at remote properties where the noise will not alert anyone. Store furniture under lock and key when not in use, and if possible secure ornaments to solid masonry. This will also help to prevent them from being stolen.

Front garden security

It is much more difficult to make your front garden secure, and in general you need to provide free access to your front door for deliveries and callers. Make sure that your front door has the highest standards of security (see pages 86 to 90) and that accessible windows are fitted with locks or other security devices (pages 94 to 99). Hang nets or café curtains at downstairs windows to deter snoopers, and install an automatic light that will come on as soon as someone sets foot on the property (see pages 118 to 121). Lastly, make sure that there is no easy access around the sides of the house to the back garden, by keeping side gates bolted and fences in good order.

If your house has a fully enclosed front garden with a high perimeter wall or fence, you could consider having a lockable gate (see below) and an intercom system linking it to the house so you can talk to callers waiting there. With this arrangement, it is a good idea to provide a lockable post-box at the gate unless someone is always available to admit the person delivering the post.

Entrance gates

If the front of your property has a boundary wall or fence, closed entrance gates may help to deter the casual intruder, but they will not stop the professional unless they are high and under lock and key or remotely controlled from the house and car. It may be worth considering this level of security if your house is well set back from the road and has a secure front boundary, but it is beyond the budget of most householders: the money would be better spent on securing the house and fitting security lighting.

Garage doors

If you have a garage, make sure that its main door and any accessible personal (side) doors are secure (see pages 101 to 102 for more details). If it is detached, fit security lighting to give it additional protection from intruders. You can make an up-and-over door more secure by installing an automatic door opener.

Estate design

If you are moving house, it pays to look for a property where good security is a feature of the area, whether by accident or design. Points to look for include:

- good **street lighting** and well-lit **footpaths**
- **parking places** in view of the property
- **cul-de-sacs** where strangers will be conspicuous
- public **footpaths** overlooked by house windows
- **back-to-back gardens** with no common rear access

- **flats** that overlook their entrances
- external **meter cupboards**.

See also Designed-in security on pages 145–6.

Security lighting

Alongside the physical security measures outlined in the previous section, there is one other powerful deterrent you can use to keep burglars away: light. Darkness is the perfect cover for the burglar, so he will not be at all keen to approach a building with good exterior lighting.

Installing the lights is quite straightforward so long as they are on the house wall, since they can be wired up as extensions of your existing indoor circuits. Lights in the grounds remote from the house must have their own circuit – a wiring job you may prefer to leave to a professional electrician.

As far as choosing how to operate the lights, you have several options. You can simply switch them on at dusk and off at dawn (if you turn them off at bedtime, you lose their deterrent effect), or fit a photoelectric switch which will do the same thing automatically. However, leaving the lights on all night uses electricity needlessly and could be relatively expensive if you use high-wattage lights. The best solution is to have the lights controlled by a movement detector which switches them on when it detects an intruder within its field of view. The sudden burst of light will be an unexpected surprise that will quickly have him scurrying for cover. A built-in timer then turns the light off again after a pre-set time, avoiding any unnecessary waste of electricity. Also, most models have a light-sensitive switch so that they operate only at night.

Planning outside lighting

To deter burglars effectively you need to light up all possible approach routes to your house. What this involves in practice depends on the layout of your house and garden; a mid-terrace house with a postage-stamp front garden obviously needs fewer outside lights than a detached house in half an acre of grounds.

Remember that outside lighting has other benefits apart from deterring burglars. It means that you do not have to approach your front door in the dark, and it shows the way for visitors too. You will be able to see your way to the dustbin, the garage or the garden shed, and even to enjoy the garden after dark. So think about where *you* need light too when planning the positions of the various fittings.

Start at the front door. You need a low-level fitting here so that you can see to unlock the door and to identify callers. Depending on the size of your front garden and the degree of illumination this light provides, you may also need a high-level light to illuminate the whole front garden, not just the vicinity of the door itself. When siting this, check that it will not be visible from the road, where it could dazzle drivers unexpectedly if the road approaches the house head-on.

At the back of the house you need a high-level light to deter anyone entering the property from that direction. You may also want less bright low-level lights which you can use to illuminate the patio or to see your way out of the back door.

If there is access down either side of your house, it pays to have lights there too, but consider your neighbours and check that the lights will not be intrusive when seen from their property. A light on the corner of the house may be able to cast its light along two adjacent walls.

Lastly, you may want light fittings away from the house too, to illuminate a long drive or front path. As mentioned earlier, these must have their own circuit unless they are the low-voltage type; the latter are in any case not really bright enough to use as security lighting. Leave the installation of mains lighting to a professional electrician unless you are sure of your ability to do the job correctly and safely.

Use a garage inspection lamp on a long lead to work out the ideal positions for the various fittings, aiming to create overlapping pools of light that eliminate any areas of shadow where a burglar could approach the house unseen.

Choosing the fittings

It goes without saying that any light fittings you choose must be suitable for outdoor use. A wide range of styles is available, from utility floodlights and bulkhead lights to highly decorative fittings and post lights. Choose decorative types for lighting up front doors and patios in low-level positions where the fitting will be a feature of the building, and more functional types installed at high level for deterring burglars.

The fittings available fall into three main groups:

- those taking a **standard tungsten lamp** (or a compact fluorescent lamp; these are ideal for outdoor use because of their long life)
- those taking **sealed spotlamps**, and
- those with a **halogen tube**.

The last type is extremely bright, and the 500-watt models on the market are really far too powerful for most properties unless they have extensive grounds. After all, you do not want to illuminate the neighbours' bedrooms every time you step outside your back door, and they will not thank you for it either. Remember that a little light goes a long way in the dark.

Choosing the controls

As mentioned earlier, you can control your outside lighting with manual or photoelectric switches, but movement detectors (PIR or passive infra-red detectors) are much more practical. You can buy special light fittings in a range of styles that incorporate their own detector, or fit a separate sensor that controls one or more lights – generally a cheaper option, especially when you already have the lights and simply want to bring them under PIR control.

When buying such detectors, either separately or combined with a light fitting, check their field of view and detection range so you can select one that suits your property. Other features to look for include the option of manual override by a separate switch, a variable lamp-on time and ease of changing the lamp.

With most movement detectors, it is possible for a burglar to sidle up to the detector and mask it without triggering the lights if he can reach the unit. He may also be able to reach and sever any surface-mounted cables. You should therefore aim to site it at least 2.4m (8ft) above ground level.

Fitting the lights

Once you have chosen the fittings and controls and decided where they are to be located, you can start work on the installation. If you have any doubts at all as far as your electrical competence is concerned, call in an electrician.

First, work out which indoor circuit you will extend to provide power for the new fittings. Check what wattage your lighting circuits are currently supplying. If they are close to their limit of 1,150 watts per circuit, you should not extend them, especially if you are running powerful floodlights. The alternative is to wire up a fused spur from one of your power circuits. If you have a separate upstairs circuit, use that; it will be less heavily loaded than the downstairs circuit, and the wiring is at a more convenient level for supplying light fittings installed at eaves level.

Take cable to each fitting through a hole drilled in the house wall, ideally immediately behind the light position so the cable will be completely concealed. Make the connections, mount the fitting on the wall and waterproof around its baseplate with silicone mastic.

If you are using a movement detector, adjust the unit to give the optimum coverage. Check that it will not be activated by pedestrians or cars passing your property.

Property outside

Your house and its contents are not the only things in danger nowadays; anything that can be moved from its surroundings is fair game for the thief with an eye to the main chance. That includes leisure or garden equipment left out in the open, and also expensive things like boats, caravans and motor bikes, both when they are on your property and, more importantly, when they are away from it. Don't forget the humble extension ladder hanging on the garden wall, either; even if a burglar cannot use it to gain access to your well-secured home, there is nothing to stop him carrying it along the road so he can use it to burgle your less well-protected neighbour.

Ladders

Unless you are able to keep ladders and steps under cover in a securely locked garage or outbuilding, fit brackets to a house or boundary wall so that you can hang them up neatly out of the way, and secure them in position so they cannot be removed.

The simplest way of doing this is to use a masonry expansion anchor fitted with a large screw eye. This fits into a hole drilled in the masonry (not into the mortar joints), and tightening the screw eye into the sleeve anchors it securely in place. You can then loop a length of security chain through the screw eye and the rungs of the ladder, and secure the ends with a strong padlock.

Garden equipment

Garden equipment, especially mowers and other power tools, is popular among the criminal fraternity since it is easy to cart off and easy to sell. Equipment has even been known to vanish from front gardens while the owner stepped inside the house for a few minutes.

Whenever possible, keep such equipment under lock and key when it is not in use, and give yourself a chance of getting it back if it is stolen and recovered by keeping a note of the make, model and serial number and, if possible, by marking it with your postcode and house number (or the first three letters of the house name if your house is not numbered). See Protecting your belongings on pages 132–8 for more details of the various methods you can use to do this.

Expensive garden furniture and elaborate garden statuary are also a target for thieves. Unless your seats and tables stay in the same place all the time (in which case you can copy local parks and bolt them down), your best course of action is to store them in a locked garage or outbuilding when they are not in use. As with garden equipment, mark each item unobtrusively with your postcode and house number, and take photographs of them.

As for garden statues, you may be able to drill holes through their bases and secure them to the masonry on which they stand using masonry anchors; however, this can spoil their looks (and affect their value too). The best advice is to avoid siting statuary in the front garden, to make sure that access to and from the back garden is through locked gates, and to pick large ornaments that will need two or three people to move them!

Bicycles

Bicycles, especially the more sophisticated and expensive mountain bikes, are another popular target for opportunist thieves. Many are stolen from children, so it is essential to teach them the importance of security and vigilance.

Start by having the bike security-marked, either at a cycle shop or at a police station. This involves having your postcode and house number indelibly marked on the frame in several places. As with other property marking, this acts both as a deterrent to a would-be thief and an aid to the police in getting it back for you.

Make sure that the bike is fitted with a security locking device whenever it is left unattended. D-shaped locks with a solid steel loop are harder to cut than chains. Pass the lock through the frame and one of the wheels, and secure it to something solid such as railings or other fixed street furniture. If the bike has a quick-release front wheel, take it off and pass the lock through it too.

If possible, select a bike with a quick-release saddle which you can take with you whenever you park the bike; few thieves will try to ride a saddleless bike, even if they manage to remove the lock. Remember to take lamps and luggage bags off too.

Lastly, take some photographs of the bike, including a close-up of the security markings, and make sure that you keep full details of the make, model and serial number. You will need these details to make an insurance claim if the bike is stolen and not recovered.

Caravans

Whether your caravan is parked in your garden or in a caravan park, keep it locked securely and fit a wheel clamp or towball lock. Secure the wheels with locking wheel nuts or a wheel clamp. If it is fully furnished, keep a detailed inventory of its contents and mark them with a security pen. If the caravan is left unattended, it is better to strip it of anything that is portable or valuable and to leave curtains, cupboards and lockers open so that a would-be thief can see there is nothing worth stealing. If you are unable to do this, at least fit a caravan alarm.

If your caravan is parked on a site or is stored in a compound, check that the site security is adequate. All caravans should be alarmed and immobilised.

It is well worth registering your caravan with the National Caravan Council*, which runs a scheme for marking the vehicle chassis and its windows with a unique vehicle identification number. All new caravans now belong to this scheme. Keep the registration documents safe – anywhere but in the caravan itself.

Good security lighting will also help to protect a caravan parked on your property; see the preceding section for more details.

Boats

If you keep a boat on your property, your first concern is to prevent someone towing it away on its trailer. You can fit a towball lock or wheel clamp, as for caravans, or secure the trailer to a sturdy anchor post set in concrete. Always remove outboard motors if possible; otherwise, bolt them securely in place and fit lockable nut shrouds to prevent tampering. Immobilise other motorised vessels by installing a key-operated switch that isolates the battery.

On the water, make it more difficult for a thief to steal even an immobilised boat by removing the tiller or chaining up the steering wheel, and by securing the sail boom to a deck fitting. Fit an approved intruder alarm with sensors that will protect cabin doors, windows and hatches, outboard motors and valuable navigation equipment. It is well worth having a system that also detects fire, gas and water ingress.

At many marinas, boat-owners may run a Boat Watch scheme along the same lines as Neighbourhood Watch for homes (see pages 144–5), and such a scheme is well worth joining so long as you are prepared to do your share of watching. An intruder alarm can often be linked by radio to the marina offices or to a central monitoring station.

Remember that small dinghies and canoes are also vulnerable when being carried on roof racks. Make sure that they are well secured to the rack.

Motorbikes

Motorbikes are a popular target for thieves, since two people can simply load them into a van or truck and cart them off. To protect yours as far as possible, whenever you park it lock it with a good-quality D-shaped bar lock or a security chain and padlock, and remove any valuables from the panniers. Take your helmet with you too. At home, park it in a garage if possible; otherwise keep it out of sight to the side or rear of your property. If you have to leave it in the street, leave it in a busy, well-lit area.

It is also worth immobilising the engine by fitting an electronic immobiliser or having a concealed switch that cuts any of the wires to the coil. You may be able to fit these devices yourself if you are familiar with your bike's electrical system; otherwise leave it to your dealer or a motorbike security expert.

The third security precaution you can take is to fit a bike alarm. Several models designed specifically for motorbikes are available, incorporating a siren, a shock sensor and a remote panic button, allowing you to sound the alarm from a distance if you see your bike being tampered with. Some alarm kits are suitable for d-i-y installation; others must be fitted professionally.

Pretending to be in

Eighty per cent of burglaries occur when no one is in the house. It therefore makes sense to do what you can to make the building appear occupied even when it is not. A would-be intruder will probably give you the benefit of the doubt and move elsewhere for less risky pickings. There are several steps you can take.

During the day

A snooping burglar cannot check every downstairs room at once by peering through the windows to see if anyone is about.

- When you go out, **close internal doors** so no one can see right through the house from any window.
- **Hang nets** or fit café curtains or slatted blinds at downstairs windows to make it more difficult for anyone to see in.
- Leave a **radio playing** loudly enough to be heard by someone at a window.

The addresses and phone numbers of organisations marked with an asterisk can be found in the address section at the back of the guide.

After dark

A house with no lights showing after dark and the curtains open is obviously unoccupied, and will always attract a prowling burglar.

- **Leave one or two lights on** indoors if you go out in daylight but will return after dark – ideally in rooms that no one can see into directly, such as the landing or a bedroom. The lights will not be obvious in daylight, and will cost only pennies to run.
- **Draw the curtains** too if you are going out at or after dusk, and leave a light on in at least one downstairs and one upstairs room as well as any outside lights. It is also worth leaving a radio playing somewhere, but do not leave a television switched on when you are out.
- If you will be away overnight or are going on holiday and you have **trustworthy neighbours**, give them a key and ask them to close the curtains and switch the hall and landing lights on at dusk, and to reverse the process in the morning. If you prefer not to hand over a key, at least tell your neighbours you will be away so they can keep an eye and ear open for anything untoward next door.
- Consider having **motorised curtain cord sets** fitted to draw the curtains automatically across vulnerable windows. The wall-mounted motor is operated by a photoelectric sensor and will close the curtains at dusk and open them at dawn.
- Use **time-switches to turn lights on and off** at intervals. Various types are available, ranging from simple plug-in devices for table lamps to permanently wired wall switches, and offer either timed on–off periods (which can be different each day with a seven-day timer) or random switching. Unless you have motorised curtain cord sets, use this type of control in rooms that no one can see in directly; a fully lit room visible from the road through open curtains is not much of a deterrent.
- Have **exterior lighting** wired to a photoelectric switch so it comes on at dusk and off at dawn. An intruder will be unwilling to approach a well-lit house even if he thinks it is empty in case he is spotted. See pages 118 to 121 for more information on outdoor security lighting.

Vetting callers

The newspapers regularly carry stories about intruders conning or forcing their way into people's homes, and the elderly and infirm are specially vulnerable. It is essential that you are able to identify callers at your front door, ideally before you open it to them, and it is wise to have some means of preventing forced entry even if you have opened the door.

If you live in a flat or maisonette, or you have a large house and cannot always reach the front door quickly for any reason, you may want to consider installing an entryphone system – either a simple type providing a voice link between householder and caller, or a closed circuit television (CCTV) system which allows the caller to be seen as well as heard. See Entryphones and CCTV below for more details.

It is worth remembering that some officials are legally allowed to demand entry to your home, whether you like it or not – see below under Rights of entry.

Identi]callers

When someone knocks or rings at your front door, never open it without checking first who is there. You can look out of a window if you have one that affords a good view of your doorstep. If you have a solid door, fit a door viewer (see page 92) so that you can check callers without them seeing you and without having to open the door. One system that is popular in some other parts of Europe is to position a mirror in such a way that you can look out of a nearby window and see the reflection of the person at the door. This is very cheap and has the advantage that the caller is unlikely to see you.

Preventing forced entry

If you open your door to a caller – because you believe you can trust him or her or you need to inspect any means of identification – you need to guard against the risk that an impostor might try to push in past you. The solution is to fit a door chain or limiter (see page 93), which holds the open door ajar but prevents forced entry.

If your home has a burglar alarm system, or one installed for an elderly or disabled person, a sensible extra precaution is to have a panic button (see page 107) connected to it and sited by the front door so that the alarm can be sounded quickly in an emergency.

Entryphones

A door entryphone is basically an intercom system. Inside the house is a telephone handset, usually wall-mounted for convenience and linked by flex to an external unit with a push-button operation containing a microphone, an amplifier and a small loudspeaker. When a caller presses the button, it sounds a buzzer on the indoor handset. Lifting the handset opens the circuit to the microphone and loudspeaker, allowing householder and caller to hear and speak to each other.

The final component of the system is optional: a remote-control door latch that is operated by a pushbutton on the indoor handset and allows the caller to push the door open. It is intended for use in blocks of flats or in house conversions with a common entrance hall, from where the caller then approaches an individual front door.

The system operates at low voltage from a small transformer located inside the house. This can take its power supply from a socket outlet or fused connection unit, or from a spur off a lighting circuit if this is more convenient.

The external unit may be flush- or surface-mounted, and is best sited to one side of the door at a height of about 1.5m (5ft) above the ground. It will be shower-resistant but probably not proof against driving rain, so take this into account when positioning it. The internal handset can be sited wherever it is most convenient. The flex linking the two units is slim multi-core telephone flex, which can be run unobtrusively between the two along skirting boards and around door architraves. The entryphone installation instructions will give full details of how to make the connections between the various components.

CCTV systems

The ultimate way of checking the identity of your visitors is to have a closed-circuit television system installed. This is an expensive option, but may be worth considering in conjunction with an intercom if the householder is elderly or disabled and cannot easily get to the door, or if vandalism is a regular problem (the camera can be linked to a video recorder to provide useful evidence against the perpetrators).

A basic CCTV system consists of a fixed-position camera, a small black and white TV monitor and a cable connecting the two. More sophisticated units use remotely operated scanning cameras which can pan from side to side and up and down, and may have a zoom lens that can be used to examine identification documents. The camera can be wall-mounted or built into an intercom unit; the former is vulnerable to vandalism and theft unless sited out of reach and protected with a wire cage. Integral camera and intercom units allow the householder to see the caller while holding a two-way conversation.

If you feel that a CCTV system is worth considering, get advice from a professional installer, who can recommend the most appropriate equipment for the situation.

Rights of entry

Anyone calling at your house on official business will carry an identity card or a distinctive pass, ideally incorporating a photograph. The problem lies in knowing whether it is genuine. Most service-providers (gas, electricity, water) will use a password known only to you and the official – telephone the relevant authority for more information. You could instead ask official callers to telephone you before they visit you. Otherwise, the best way of checking this is to ask the caller to wait outside while you telephone the organisation concerned and ask for verification of the name and serial number on the card. If possible, look up the organisation in the telephone directory yourself as you may simply have been given the number of an accomplice. Other signs that help to prove a caller is genuine are a uniform and a distinctively marked vehicle. If you are in any doubt, play safe and deny them admittance, however persistent they are.

As mentioned earlier, certain officials have the right to demand entry to your home whether you want them in or not, and it is in your best interests to know who they are. This checklist will help you to sort the official from the officious.

Bailiffs

A bailiff may call at your house to enforce a court judgement against you – for the non-payment of a fine, for example. You do not have to let him in unless he has a warrant of execution, and he must not use force to gain entry against your will. A warrant of execution allows him to seize goods to be sold to pay your debt.

Customs and Excise officials

Customs officers have the right to enter your home at any time to search for smuggled goods, illegal drugs or firearms if they have reasonable suspicion that such goods are on the premises. They can also force entry if they are seeking evidence of a suspected VAT fraud.

Emergency services

The employees of gas and water companies have the right of entry in the event of a gas or water leak inside your premises, and can use force to break in if necessary. Fire-fighters can also break in if they think a fire has broken out, to carry out a rescue or to gain access to a neighbouring property to fight a fire.

Inland Revenue officials

Inland Revenue staff must have a warrant obtained from a judge to enter a house when investigating serious tax fraud. They can use force if necessary, and can then remove any evidence they require (for which they should issue a receipt).

Landlords

A landlord has no general right of entry to your home if you are legally classed as a tenant, but is allowed to inspect the property to see if repairs are necessary. To do so he must give at least 24 hours' notice and call at a reasonable time of day. If you refuse access, he could obtain a court injunction; do it repeatedly and you could face eviction proceedings.

Local authority officials

Environmental health officers (EHOs) can enter your property to check for evidence of structural instability, overcrowding or fitness for habitation. They will normally give you 24 hours' notice. If you refuse them admittance, they can apply for a warrant allowing them to force entry.

Social workers have no general right of entry, but can require it if they are accompanied by police and carry a specific court authority – for example, a warrant to remove a child at risk.

The police

The police have the right to enter and search your home for a variety of reasons, including searching for stolen goods, drugs or evidence of a serious offence – a murder weapon, for example. To do this they must have a search warrant; they must give you a copy of it if you are present, and must leave a copy behind if you are not there and they have to force entry. They can enter your property without a warrant in order to make an arrest, to chase an escaped prisoner or to stop someone getting hurt.

If the police use force to enter empty premises, they must leave the building secure when they leave.

TV licence inspectors

Licence enquiry officers have no legal right of entry, but if they suspect that you are using an unlicensed television and you refuse them entry they can apply to a local magistrates' court for a search warrant. They will then return in the company of a police officer to execute the warrant.

Utility companies

Unless there is an emergency (see above), utility company staff must have your permission to enter your home to read meters, inspect fittings or disconnect your gas or electricity supply because of unpaid bills (telephone services are disconnected at the local exchange, and water at a point outside the home). If you refuse them entry, they can obtain a warrant allowing them to force entry after giving you appropriate notice. After forcing an entry, they must leave the premises secure and make good (or pay for) any damage caused.

Other callers

You are more likely to be 'doorstepped' by any of a wide range of unofficial callers than by members of the 'official' list above. None has any right of entry to your home, but some – sales representatives in particular – can be difficult to shift if you do decide to let them in.

Tell any caller who will not leave when asked to do so that he or she is trespassing and insist that he or she leave immediately. If the caller does not go, telephone the police.

Be alert to the risks mentioned earlier of tricksters posing as officials or, sad to say, groups of children wanting a 'lost ball' back. The golden rule is: if in doubt, keep them out. Genuine officials will always return, and you can tell children to wait outside a closed door while you find the ball and bring it to them.

The local police are always keen to give talks on home security to clubs and other groups of people. Some local talking newspapers for visually handicapped people can supply audio cassettes on home security.

Protecting your belongings

Unless your house is now an impenetrable fortress, you have to accept that a burglar could still gain entry somehow, sometime, and you should take a few further steps to minimise the loss or damage you might sustain as a result. There is little you can do to halt the mindless vandalism that accompanies many break-ins, but some sensible precautions can prevent the loss of certain valuables, help the police find stolen property and give you extra peace of mind.

Everyday precautions

Nothing will attract an opportunist thief more quickly than the sight of small portable valuables left tantalisingly visible within the home. It can take him only a few seconds to break in, snatch what he can and disappear again.

● Do not leave **wallets, handbags, credit cards or loose cash** on show, and avoid keeping large amounts of cash in the house.
● Keep **jewellery** you are not wearing in a fabric roll or jewellery

box, and store it somewhere accessible to you but unexpected to a burglar.

● Store favourite target **valuables** such as cameras or camcorders, portable stereos, binoculars, hand-held computer games (and their expensive game cartridges) and so on out of sight. They will be found by a burglar with time to look for them but will not attract the smash-and-grab opportunist. See below for information on computer security.

● Try to position **home entertainment equipment** out of sight of windows facing the street. Even at night their illuminated control panels can give their presence away to someone peering through an uncurtained window.

● Make sure that you are properly insured; see Chapter 4 for more information about **home insurance.**

Marking your property

While most stolen property is never recovered, you can give yourself – and the police – a chance by marking things so that they can be returned to you if they are found. By displaying a notice in your window stating that your property is security-marked, you may even deter a thief from trying to steal what he may not be able to sell easily.

The police recommend the use of your postcode plus your house number (or the first three letters of its name if it is unnumbered), since this combination is unique and proves beyond any doubt where the stolen property came from. The mark can be visible or invisible; the latter is better because the thief may miss it, while he can attempt to remove visible identification.

Invisible marking
You can put invisible marks on any item with a special security pen. The ink it uses is invisible to the naked eye when dry, but shows up clearly under ultra-violet (UV) light. Because of this, you can put the mark anywhere on the item, but concealing it somewhere unusual reduces the chance of the thief spotting it even if he has a UV light himself. You can use it for any item, but it is especially suitable for some valuable antiques where other marking methods might impair them and reduce their value. The ink can fade with time, especially if the item marked is washed, so you might consider buying a small

UV lamp for checking the marks from time to time and renewing them as necessary.

Visible marking

There are several methods you can use to put visible security marking on valuable items, including engraving, indelible marking, etching and stamping.

Engraving involves using either a carbide or diamond-tipped pen or a small electric-powered tool to carve the security marking on to the surface of the item. Both are sold with a sheet of letter and number stencils to enable you to engrave the marks neatly and legibly. Use engraving for any object with a hard, smooth surface – cameras, video recorders and so on – but avoid marking expensive glass or china in this way or you will drastically reduce its value. Place the marks where they are visible but unobtrusive; then even if the thief attempts to remove or deface the marking, its existence will show that the property is stolen and will make it less easy for him to sell.

Indelible marking is best for valuable glass and china, and also for expensive items of clothing such as leather jackets that are a popular target for thieves. Put the mark on a concealed surface using a special pen.

Etching involves the use of acid to mark the article; dry-transfer stencils are positioned on the surface of the article to mask off the security code and then acid is brushed over them to etch the area around the code. This method is used mainly for etching registration numbers on car windows; you can buy kits and do the job yourself or ask a garage or mobile marking service to do it for you.

Stamping involves the use of letter and number dies to imprint the security code, and is used mainly on metal surfaces – tools, d-i-y and garden equipment and bicycle frames. You can buy the stamps, but they are expensive and not widely available. Most police crime prevention units will stamp bicycles for you, as will many cycle shops; you can also take anything else you want stamped along to the latter.

Do not use any visible marking techniques on valuable jewellery or other gold and silver items. It is better to photograph them instead (see below).

Finally, keep a record of the make, model and serial numbers of all electrical equipment in the house. This will not only make a subsequent insurance claim simpler to authenticate, but it will also allow you to prove ownership of recovered property even if your security marks have been tampered with.

Photographing property

The best way of keeping a record of items you cannot put security marks on is to take colour photographs of them. This is especially suitable for jewellery and valuable antiques and pieces of furniture. Place the item on or against a plain background, and take pictures from several angles. Include close-ups of unusual features such as crests, initials or hallmarks if your camera can take such close-up shots. For small items, include in the picture a ruler or some other object such as a coin that will give an idea of the scale of the item you are photographing.

If you own a camcorder, it is worth making a 'home' video of your house and its contents. This will not only help jog your memory about items that may have been stolen during a break-in or damaged in a fire; it will also provide a valuable record for insurance purposes if you have to make a claim for loss or damage. Film the contents of cupboards, wardrobes and drawers too.

Storing records

Most people automatically store written or photographic records of their property in the house. However, such records could easily be lost (or even stolen by a really thorough thief). It is therefore best to place a copy of the information elsewhere – with a relative, in a bank safe-deposit box or with your insurance company, for example. Alternatively, you could consider installing a safe, where you could also keep cash and small valuables such as jewellery.

Home safes

A safe is the ultimate line of protection for your property, but in practical terms can store only relatively small items and is best used for cash, jewellery and irreplaceable papers such as property deeds (although the latter may be safer in a bank or commercial safe deposit – see below).

What type of safe you choose will depend on the degree of security you require. First of all, consider whether you are more concerned about burglary or fire. A burglar-proof safe has a thick steel body, sophisticated locks and hardened security bolts, but papers stored inside it may char in a fire. A fireproof safe has a lighter-duty twin-wall construction lined with insulation material to protect documents inside it, but is not so secure against physical attack.

It is also worth contacting your household insurance company for advice if you plan to install a safe. They will advise you on the level of security you need, which depends on the value of the items you want to store in it. Some insurers may not regard d-i-y installation as satisfactory and will insist on professional fitting.

Mini-safes

The least expensive type of safe is a small container designed to fit in a recess in a wall or floor. The safe may be in the form of a tube or a rectangular box, and provides a hiding-place rather than any serious burglar resistance. Most are intended to be concealed from view – behind a picture or beneath a carpet – but one is designed to resemble a double electrical socket outlet, with the faceplate acting as the safe door. A mini-safe is worth considering if you want to hide a small volume of valuables without vast expense.

Strong-boxes

These are reinforced metal boxes designed to be screwed (or preferably bolted) to the floor or to the base of a cupboard – a wardrobe, for example. They offer more storage space than a mini-safe, and give a reasonable degree of protection if they are well concealed and carefully sited so that tools cannot easily be used to force them.

Freestanding safes

If you want reasonable security for more or bulkier items without any installation problems, the best choice is a freestanding safe. This is secured to the floor from within the safe to prevent a thief from lifting and removing it. A range of sizes is available, from a small television-sized box to a fridge-sized cupboard. The drawback with a freestanding safe is its utilitarian appearance, but it can be sited within a cupboard. On the other hand, you can easily take it with you when you move house, which you cannot do easily (if at all) with other types of safe.

Wall safes

A wall safe is basically a strongly reinforced steel cupboard that is built into a masonry wall. The wall thickness obviously restricts the depth of the safe to a maximum of about 125mm (5in); the height and width are usually multiples of standard brick sizes to make installation easy. To prevent a thief from trying to chop out and remove the safe, most incorporate side lugs or projecting bolts that lock the safe into the masonry once it has been installed.

It is obviously sensible to conceal a wall safe from view. Use the classic Hollywood method of hanging a picture or mirror over it if it has no projecting locks; this allows you easy access to the safe, so is ideal if you use it regularly. If you do not, conceal it behind furniture or bookshelves.

Floor safes

Floor safes, as their name implies, are designed to be installed in suspended timber or solid concrete floors; the latter type offers the highest level of protection, against fire as well as burglary. The safe consists of a square or round chamber fitted with a strong lockable lid which is generally concealed beneath a cover plate. Types for suspended timber floors are usually designed to be bolted in place between adjacent joists. Types for concrete floors are more difficult to install, since the floor has to be excavated and the hole damp-proofed before the safe can be concreted into place. This type can also be installed beneath timber floors if there is room for the safe to be surrounded by timber formwork and then encased in concrete.

Banks and commercial safe deposits

Most banks offer safe-deposit facilities. What they charge for the service will depend on the size of the package or deed box you want stored, and on how frequently you need access to it. Since you can use such a service only during banking hours, it is best kept for storing documents which you need only rarely. Make sure you get a receipt for whatever you deposit.

Commercial safe-deposit companies (and some banks) offer safety-deposit boxes. These are locked and kept in secure vaults, and only you know what is in the box. You pay according to the size of box you need and the number of times you need access. Opening hours are generally longer than a bank's – more convenient if you want to store valuable jewellery that you might want to take out and return in the same evening.

Computer security

More and more households now have a home computer, which may be used for educational, entertainment or business purposes (or a permutation of all three). Such equipment, plus its associated software, is particularly attractive to burglars because it is relatively portable and very easy to sell. It is therefore worth paying special attention to its physical security, over and above any precautions you may take to secure your home against intruders. The lure of equipment worth hundreds or thousands of pounds, especially if it is on view through a window, could be hard for a knowledgeable thief to resist.

If you have a home computer, be sure to inform your household contents insurance company, especially if the equipment is for business use. They may well insist on your taking additional security precautions before they will agree to cover it.

Your home computer is also at risk from another threat: viruses. These can be imported into the system on disks from other computer users, and if the computer is linked to others, as many homeworkers' computers are, the virus can contaminate the entire network. The loss of irreplaceable data due to a virus can be annoying at best and, in the case of business data, extremely expensive and time-consuming.

Physical security

There is now a wide range of security products specially designed to protect computer equipment. Most have been developed for use in commercial premises where computer theft is now endemic, but they are suitable for home use too.

The simplest use steel-cored cables to secure the equipment to the surface it sits on, or to a nearby wall or floor. A pad is bonded to the casing of each piece of equipment with strong adhesive; the cable is looped through the pad, run to a secure plate fixed to the wall or floor pad and then secured to it with a padlock. This type of security is ideal if the equipment needs to be moved around on the work-surface, and the padlocks can simply be released if necessary to allow the equipment to be transferred to another location.

A higher degree of security is provided by a range of fittings that includes baseplates, rail locks and equipment enclosures:

- To use a **baseplate**, you stick special fixing feet to the base of the equipment and then bolt them to the upper section of the baseplate; this is itself mounted and locked to the work-surface.
- **Rail locks** are two-part fixings, one of which is secured to the equipment and one to the work-surface; you simply release the lock to free the equipment.
- **Enclosures** provide the highest level of security. You secure the casing to the work-surface, place the equipment on a sliding tray, push it into the enclosure and lock the tray in place. This avoids the need to stick or bolt anything to the equipment itself. The enclosure can also be fitted with a locking front plate that prevents access to the floppy disk drive or to front-mounted switches.

When deciding on the level of security you want, remember that it is the computer itself, rather than the monitor or keyboard, which is of most value to a thief. Secure that and you should be safe. You can also use the cable-and-pad method to secure expensive television and stereo equipment in the home.

You may be able to obtain these security devices from your computer supplier, but few are as yet prepared to offer their customers these essential accessories despite their comparatively low cost. Your best bet is to contact your insurance company for details of an approved security equipment manufacturer, or else to ask your local Crime Prevention Officer.

There are two other simple steps you can take to protect your computer equipment. The first is to mark each item with your postcode and house number, as you would other high-value items in your home. You can use an ultra-violet security pen, a permanent ink marker or a scriber to do this; it is also a good idea to stick an anti-thief warning label on the equipment to warn that it is marked. The second step is to fit an audible alarm to the equipment, ideally inside the casing (ask your dealer or security firm). Small electronic alarms measuring only 38 x 38 x 25mm (1½ x 1½ x 1in) will fit inside most pieces of equipment, and will trigger a loud alarm if the equipment is moved once the alarm has been armed.

The last security measure you should take will not save your equipment from being stolen by a determined thief, but will at least safeguard the data stored on it. It is the simple but often-ignored action of keeping systems disks and copies of all data disks away from the machine location in a secure place. There are important reasons for doing this:

- to stop it being **stolen and pirated**
- to **prevent other members of the family** reading your private letters and other files
- to keep safe **sensitive business data** that you are working on at home.

If you are burgled, you will then at least be able to get back to work, do the household accounts or finish your novel as soon as you can get hold of replacement equipment. Keep your back-up disks, plus all your original software disks, somewhere well away from the computer itself.

Keeping viruses at bay

If you use a stand-alone computer and never run disks from other computer users, you can reasonably expect to avoid infection by a computer virus. However, if you do swap disks, use an electronic bulletin-board service or are linked to a computer network, the risk of infection is very real.

You can use one of the many virus detection and elimination programs to check your system. Even if you do not appear to have any problems at present with the way your computer works or with the information on your disks, it pays to check as regularly as is practicable. Do so:

- **before using or copying information** from any disk, even commercial software
- **before copying in any files from a network** or from information services or bulletin-boards

- **before sending information** on disks or electronically to other users.

New viruses appear regularly, so make sure you have the latest version of the virus detection program to ensure complete protection. Use only one program at a time to avoid compatibility problems.

Personal security

The *fear* of danger and physical attack is a very real one nowadays, especially among women, elderly people and those who live alone. Although the statistical risk of you or a member of your family being attacked in or around the house is small, it is well worth taking some simple precautions.

Security at home

Although locks and other security devices are primarily intended to protect your home when you are out, one in five burglaries takes place in occupied premises. It therefore makes sense to use the locks and other devices when you are at home too.

For a start, keep external doors locked, and at least close all windows at the front of the house in unoccupied rooms, especially if you are in the garden. At night, draw the curtains and close and lock all windows, except those in bedrooms if you need some ventilation. Many modern window frames incorporate ventilation slots that can be used without opening the window (although they provide only background ventilation). Otherwise, if a window is accessible from outside, either fit locks that allow the window to be opened slightly for ventilation, or fit a security bar or grille across it to deny anyone access. Use your burglar alarm system to monitor the downstairs zone when you go to bed if it has zone control.

See the earlier section on Vetting callers for advice on checking the credentials of anyone you do not recognise. Do not allow your children to answer the front door on their own.

What if you're burgled?

If you return to your home and find that it has been burgled, telephone the police immediately. Do not touch anything except to

141

minimise damage – turning off a tap that has been left running to stop an overflow, for example. Start to itemise everything that appears to have been stolen, so that when the scene-of-crime officer arrives you can help him or her to complete the crime report form quickly and accurately. See Chapter 4 on insurance for advice on claiming for loss and/or damage on your insurance policies.

If you arrive home and discover signs that suggest a break-in may be in progress – an open door or window, or a strange van parked outside with some of your possessions loaded into the back – do not approach or enter the house. Go to a neighbour's house, or to a telephone box if there is one nearby, and telephone the police from there. The police normally react very quickly if someone reports a burglary in progress. Then keep a discreet eye on the house so you can give the police a description of anyone leaving the building.

If you get indoors and then find an intruder in the house, ask calmly what he wants and then tell him to leave: getting angry may provoke a violent reaction. Do not attempt to restrain him, and do not fight over any stolen property he may be holding. Try to memorise his appearance in as much detail as possible, then call the police and write the details down as soon as he has left. If you can, record his age, height, build, skin colour, hair colour and style, facial characteristics and clothing. If he uses a vehicle, try to note the type, model, colour and as much of the registration number as you can. Photograph it if you have a camera to hand.

If you suspect that there is a prowler outside your house at any time, call the police. At night-time, turn lights on and make a noise upstairs to scare the intruder away, and look out from upstairs windows to try to see what he looks like and which direction he takes when he leaves. Do not venture downstairs if you suspect that someone is actually inside the house, or is still there despite your noisy warnings. Select something you can use as a weapon to defend yourself in case you are attacked. Call the police if you have a telephone upstairs, or hit the panic button if one is part of your burglar alarm system. An elderly person with a community alarm can use that to summon help in this situation.

Remember that once you have been burgled, your chances of being burgled again can increase. The thieves already know how best to get in and may return for things they could not carry the first time. They may even wait for you to replace the stolen items and then come back for those too. To be safe, make good any damage they have caused and plug any remaining security weak spots immediately.

Telephone security

Nuisance calls, whether from cold-call telesales staff or heavy-breathing perverts, have always been a risk to all telephone subscribers. Having an ex-directory number will keep telesales staff at bay, or else you can register with the Telephone Preference Service. Phone 0800 398893 (BT customers) or 0500 398893 (Mercury customers) for an application form. Customers of other companies should find the appropriate number on their phone bills.

British Telecom has recently introduced a caller identification service which in theory should help to put an end to the phenomenon of the nuisance caller. This enables you to obtain the telephone number of the last call you received by dialling 1471 – something an obscene caller would not want you to know – and to report it to the police.

However, the system works both ways. If you are making a call and do not want your number revealed, you can preface the call by dialling 141, and you can arrange to have your number permanently withheld by dialling 0800 801471. Unfortunately, so can anyone calling you. So if you receive unidentifiable malicious or obscene calls, all you can do is report them to the police; the caller's number will have been retained at the telephone exchange even though it was barred to you, and BT will continue to trace such callers at police request. Note that this service is not available on some older mobile phones or some cable systems.

Do not give out your number when answering the phone. If a stranger calls, do not admit that you are on your own. Put the phone down immediately if the call is abusive or obscene, or else quietly place the handset by the side of the phone, leave the room for a few minutes, and replace the phone later. Any persistent caller will soon learn that he or she is talking into thin air. If you want your telephone number listed in the directory, display only your surname and initials so a stranger will not know whether the occupant is male or female.

If you use a telephone answering machine, word your message to indicate that you are busy rather than out of the house, and don't give your name and number in the message.

Security outdoors

When you are out and about, stay alert for any signs of impending danger. If it makes you feel safer, carry a personal alarm in your hand so that you can operate it instantly if necessary. Gas-operated alarms are generally louder than battery ones but can freeze up and fall silent after a few minutes. Electronic types are more reliable and sound for an acceptable time, but are more expensive than gas types. No system should exceed 130 decibels. Choose a type that locks on when operated so that it will continue to sound even if you drop it.

See Street safety on pages 164–6 for more advice on keeping out of danger when you are out and about.

Shared security

You have now done all you can yourself to protect your home, its occupants and its contents. The last line of defence is to involve the whole neighbourhood in fighting crime in your area by getting everyone to keep their eyes and ears open and to report any suspicious behaviour to the police. You can of course do this on an informal basis, but it is likely to be more effective if organised professionally as a Neighbourhood Watch scheme.

How Neighbourhood Watch works

Neighbourhood Watch is an idea that originated in San Francisco and was first introduced to this country in 1982. Its title is self-explanatory; apart from its main aim of deterring criminals, it helps to make its members more aware of security matters generally and can also help to foster a sense of community that is often lacking nowadays as people become more private in their lifestyles.

The scheme is masterminded by local police Crime Prevention Officers (CPOs), who will tell you if there is one operating already in your area and give you advice on setting one up if there is not. For the scheme to work you need the agreed co-operation of a majority of your neighbours, and someone keen to act as the area co-ordinator. If a residents' association or similar community group already exists, the Neighbourhood Watch scheme can build on that.

Once you have recruited interested members, the local CPO will attend a home meeting, deliver a talk (or show a video) about the scheme and give general advice on home and personal security matters. He or she will also provide leaflets about the scheme and stickers to display in the windows of participating houses – a small but worthwhile additional security device – and will organise the provision and erection of street signs which announce that the area is a Neighbourhood Watch zone, another visual deterrent to criminals.

On a day-to-day basis, the scheme needs proper organisation so that members know whom to contact for advice and how to report anything suspicious. It is best to divide the area up into small zones containing just a few houses, each with its own block co-ordinator who should ideally be at home most of the time. These people field calls from other members and pass them on if necessary both to the police and to the area co-ordinator; the latter is chiefly responsible for keeping up enthusiasm for the scheme among the participants by holding regular meetings, circulating newsletters and so on. Without that enthusiasm, the scheme will soon fall into disuse and its effectiveness will be greatly reduced.

Designed-in security

Apart from Neighbourhood Watch, there is another 'shared' security approach which applies to new housing developments and which is worth looking out for if you are planning to buy a new house. It is called Secured by Design, and is an initiative to reduce crime on new developments both at the design and estate planning stage and on completion, creating homes with a high level of integral security. It is jointly sponsored by the police, the insurance companies, house developers and suppliers of security hardware, and has Home Office backing.

To be allowed to use the Secured by Design name and logo, a developer must prove that the particular scheme satisfies a range of security requirements. The estate itself should have the following features:

- a strong **perimeter fence**, especially where it adjoins open spaces, roads and railways
- **cul-de-sacs** rather than through roads, to keep non-residents away and to make strangers appear more conspicuous

- **footpaths** that are overlooked by house windows
- **back-to-back gardens** where access is limited and visibility from the house is good
- **parking places** where owners can keep an eye on their own vehicles and those of any visitors
- **boundary fences** or **walls** that are hard to climb
- good **street lighting** and **well-lit footpaths**
- **flats** that overlook their entry areas
- **planting** and **site landscaping** which do not provide cover for criminal activity.

The houses themselves should have a high level of built-in security, including the following:

- **automatic deadlocks** or **mortise deadlocks** on all exterior doors
- **locks at the top and bottom of patio doors**
- **locks on all downstairs windows** and on any other windows where access is possible
- **windows with limiters** so that they will not open by more than about 150mm (6in) unless the limiter is released
- **stout doors and locks on garages and sheds**
- **gas and electricity meters in external cupboards** so that they can be read from outside the house
- **exterior lights** that can be controlled from inside the house
- wiring for a **burglar alarm system** installed as an integral part of the house.

CHAPTER 3

SECURITY AND SAFETY OUTSIDE THE HOME

Car security

Car crime has become one of the big growth areas of the 1990s, accounting for over a quarter of all recorded crime in the UK. The statistics make grim reading: one car is stolen every minute; a theft from a car happens every 35 seconds; in a year, 1 in 25 cars has something stolen from it; and 1 in 40 is actually stolen. A report published by the RAC in May 1994 put England and Wales at the top of the international car-crime league, even above the USA.

Cars are stolen for three main purposes. By far the most significant, accounting for around two-thirds of thefts, is for one-off use. This includes 'joy-riding', stealing a car to use in another crime or simply taking a car to get home after the last bus has left. Many of these stolen vehicles are dumped a few hours later.

Around a quarter of cars are stolen by 'professional' thieves. The cars either go through an identity change (known as 'ringing') before being sold on, or are stripped down for their spare parts. Finally, a proportion of cars that have been reported as stolen, are, in fact, being used by the owners in an attempt to defraud their insurance companies. This is more common with older cars which have become less economic to repair for the MOT or after an accident.

Security improvements in new cars

Over the years the security of newly designed cars has gradually been improved. Unfortunately, the thief has, by and large, managed to discover ways around most forms of new protection. This is particularly true of steering column locks, which were hailed as a great step forward when introduced, but quickly became just another hindrance which was simple to overcome. Since 1992, however, many new models have been fitted with security features which may prove far more effective. The key features you should look for in a new car are given below.

Central door locking
This has one major advantage: as long as you remember to lock the driver's door the rest of the car will be locked too. This may sound obvious, but drivers still forget to lock their cars fully when leaving them.

Deadlocks
A deadlock has the normal key-operated locking position, plus an additional high security one. Ordinary door locks can sometimes be overcome by tampering with the mechanism inside the door – it is no secret that thieves enter cars by poking a tool between the window and door frame and fiddling around until the lock releases. A deadlocked car generally resists such attacks much better than a traditional lock. More importantly, you cannot open a deadlocked car from inside, so the casual thief who smashes a window to reach the locks inside will not be able to open a door (though he may still be able to reach the radio or personal belongings).

There have been some worries that young children who may have been locked into a car by their parents to keep them safe while shopping could then not be released in an emergency. For this reason, many car manufacturers force you to operate the deadlock positively by making an extra turn of the key – otherwise only the standard locks will be in operation. While this has its advantages, it does mean that for your car to be fully secure at all times you must make sure you deadlock it properly before leaving it. Some cars allow you to do this by remote control.

Alarms
Car alarms fall into two categories – those approved by the car manufacturer itself, and those sold as accessories for any make of car; the accessory side is covered later (see under Adding security to your car).

It has become increasingly common for car manufacturers to incorporate an alarm into the design of the car. That is a good idea, because all the complicated electrical wiring can be hidden away as the car is built, increasing both security and reliability. A built-in alarm is also a favoured option because every car manufacturer will try to make sure that the alarm works well: it is not in the manufacturer's interests to have an alarm system which is prone to going off at the wrong time. So you can reckon that any factory-fitted car alarm should offer a reasonable level of protection, even if it is not the latest thing in terms of sophistication and features. Many car manufacturers, however, particularly importers from the Far East, rely upon their dealers to fit the alarm. In theory, you should also get a good job if you take this route, though you need to check that the dealer really does fit an alarm system approved by the importer, rather than one available more cheaply elsewhere. There is nothing wrong with accessory alarms from independent sources, but you should feel more reassured if you know the alarm has been tried out before in your particular model of car.

Electronic immobilisers

This is a more recent innovation than the car alarm. An immobiliser is installed into a car's wiring system so that it is (in theory) impossible to start the engine without the correct device. Usually this is a small additional key with a coded microchip – you insert the key into a socket in the dashboard each time you want to start the engine. On certain cars there is a key-pad, where you have to key in a secret number to override the immobiliser, or it may be operated by remote control.

The virtue of the immobiliser over the standard ignition cut-out which is incorporated into many alarm systems is that it is much more difficult to overcome. The wiring is usually designed to be extremely confusing for a potential thief, so that even if the wires are cut and re-routed, the chances of getting the engine going are very small.

Only a few manufacturers fit immobilisers to their cars as standard, but the number is likely to increase. Ford has introduced a system where the electronic chip is built into the ignition key, so that each time you insert the key the immobiliser is de-activated. There are several companies on the market fitting immobilisers as optional extras.

Vehicle identification

Every car has its own vehicle identification number (VIN) which is displayed in the engine compartment. A recent security development is 'visible VIN', where a plate is securely bonded into an inaccessible but visible position (usually under the base of the windscreen). The idea is that if the car is stolen and 'ringed', it is extremely difficult to change all the identifying tags throughout the car, so a potential buyer merely has to make sure that VIN numbers are all the same.

A development of this is to print the VIN on a large number of microdots, about the size of a pin-head. These are then scattered throughout the car during manufacture. If a car is thought to be stolen, these can be located with a special detector and checked to see that all the numbers correlate. Obviously, this is far from foolproof, but it does require an enormous amount of tedious work on behalf of the thieves to overcome. This development is confined to luxury cars, where it may be offered as an option.

Secure stereo systems

The car stereo remains an attraction for many opportunist thieves, despite the fact that it is difficult to comprehend why there should still be a strong market for stolen stereos. With some form of radio cassette fitted to nearly every car sold in the UK, the car manufacturers and radio suppliers have developed three main ways to combat stereo theft: security coding, the removable stereo system and the 'unique' stereo.

Security coding has been available for some time. A radio with this feature will not work if the power is cut from it – when it is removed from the car – without the correct code being punched back in. To prevent a thief merely going through all the available numbers in order to arrive at the correct code, the security system will often let you have only half a dozen tries to get it right before refusing to accept any more attempts for several hours. Although a sound idea in principle, it seems that there are ways of getting round the coding by anyone with the right electronic equipment.

A more secure alternative is the **removable stereo system**. The set has a small handle built in, allowing the complete unit to be slid from the dashboard and taken with you or secreted elsewhere in the car. Unfortunately, most radios are too heavy to carry around comfortably, so drivers, when they do remember to remove them, tuck them under the front seat or in the boot. Thieves know this and may chance a break-in even when there is obviously a hole in the dashboard where the stereo should be.

A more satisfactory alternative is the **removable front panel**. The idea is the same, but with these you merely unclip a portion of the front of the stereo about the size of a comb, and slip it into your pocket. Replacements for these are so expensive that it is not worth the trouble of stealing the rest of the unit.

Then there is the **unique stereo**. This has to be designed into the car from the outset, and its unique layout, often with the controls quite separate from the display, means that it will not fit any other model of car. This is a very strong deterrent as there is absolutely no point in stealing a stereo that can be fitted only into the same model of car, which almost certainly has the same system already.

Finally, retractable aerials offer valuable protection against vandals and car washes.

Adding security to your car

There are literally hundreds of devices available to protect your car, from sophisticated items costing £500 which have to be installed by a specialist, to simple locks which can be bought for under £20. Which you choose will depend not only on the depth of your pocket but also the risk you feel your car runs of being attacked or stolen.

Alarms

The cost of car alarms varies enormously – you can buy products under this general description for £30 or £500. So what can you expect, and which features are the important ones to go for?

The dominant feature of every alarm is that it makes a loud noise. At the very cheapest end of the market, this noise might be the sort which is unpleasant for the thief rather than attracting others' attention. There are very easy-to-fit devices with built-in batteries which lock over the steering wheel or are fixed to the dashboard. When the car is entered, a change in air pressure will set off the internal siren, which is supposed to make it unbearable for the thief to drive away. When *Which?* tested two of these devices in November 1992 it found they were easy for the determined thief to detach and throw out.

More effective alarms are wired into the car's electrical system and will sound a siren under the bonnet to deter the intruder. They range from the simple units operated by a hidden switch inside the car which sound the alarm perhaps 10 seconds after a door has been opened, to devices that detect movement inside the car and are switched on and off by remote control.

When selecting an alarm for your car you should first consider whether you are going to fit it yourself (in which case you will probably be looking for a relatively simple system) or get the job done professionally. Then make up your mind about which of the following features you feel are necessary. By and large the more you have, the higher the level of security.

Engine immobilisation is an important ingredient, preventing the engine from being started when the alarm is in operation.

A **back-up battery** means that even if the thief disconnects or cuts wiring to the car battery, the alarm will still operate – indeed, it will probably go off as soon as the car battery is taken out of the electrical circuit.

A car alarm which is operated by **remote control** is more secure than the type with a hidden switch. When you buy the car, check the number of remote controllers you will get if there is more than one driver. Many will also operate the car's central locking at the same time, so check whether this feature is available – it is not universal. Some remote-control systems automatically change their code each time they are operated in order to impede 'grabbers'. These devices are used by thieves to pick up the signal from your remote control as you operate it; they then copy it electronically into their own remote.

An alarm may have several different types of sensor built into it, or come with just one with others offered as optional extras. A **direct contact sensor** works in the same way as the switches in the door which control the interior light. **Voltage drop sensors** sense when any electric equipment, such as the starter motor, is switched on. They can cause false alarms in cars where the cooling fan on the engine runs after the engine has been switched off. **Current sensors** work in a similar way but monitor only the current drawn by certain circuits.

All of these rely upon a change in the car's electrical system being detected. **Ultrasonic detectors**, on the other hand, sense changes in air pressure within the car caused by movement. This is a good principle, but is the main cause of so many alarms sounding unnecessarily on a windy day, when air gets through the vents into the car and causes a disturbance. The trick is to shut these vents (and the windows and sunroof) when you leave the car.

Shock sensors detect a sudden movement of the car - if it is bumped, for example. A **tilt sensor** will sound if the car is lifted up to be towed away, or jacked up to remove the wheels.

A **panic mode** on the alarm will allow you to set off the alarm from inside the car in an emergency, or possibly from outside if you see someone trying to break in. Some alarms will **report back**, which means you will get an indication that the alarm had gone off while you were away from the car.

Finally, make sure the alarm offers a good visual deterrent to any potential criminal. After all, it is better for the thief to be deterred *before* attempting to break in rather than after, when the alarm sounds.

Note that the insurance industry tests car security devices (various types of alarms and immobilisers) for approval to its own set of standards of reliability and security. You can obtain a copy of the latest results (and updates) by sending a large stamped addressed envelope to the Association of British Insurers.*

Electronic immobilisers

The immobilisers described earlier can be fitted to almost any make of car. Most have more than one way of preventing a car from being started, and a thief has to overcome all of them. They are expensive. They do not, of course, prevent a determined thief loading your car on a trailer and taking it away to deal with the immobiliser elsewhere. Nor do they usually include any form of alarm.

Clamps and locks

A vast range of clamps exists, providing a mechanical and visual deterrent to stealing a car. The two most popular are the **steering wheel-to-pedal lock**, which locks the wheel to the clutch or brake pedal, and the **steering wheel clamp**, which comprises a large steel bar locked to the steering wheel to obstruct its movement.

You can also buy **wheel clamps**, superficially like those used to clamp your car for a parking offence, a **gearlever lock** and **gear-to-handbrake lock**. When *Which?* tested a wide range of mechanical clamps and locks in November 1992 it overcame almost all of them by force or with a few simple tools. Only three scored an acceptable rating for security, and most were poor or worse. Their main value is as a visual deterrent to opportunist thieves.

Locking wheel nuts

Expensive alloy wheels are an easy target, but can easily be protected with locking wheel nuts. These usually come in sets of four – one locking nut for each wheel – and are easy to fit and use. You *must* remember to keep the key with you in case you have a puncture.

Window etching

Getting all the separate pieces of glass in your car windows etched with the car's registration number is a cheap and easy way to deter the more serious thief. Each piece of glass is indelibly marked with the registration number. To disguise a stolen car for sale, a thief then has to replace the glass as well, a costly and time-consuming business.

Tracker

A new car theft measure is the Tracker system, sold through the Automobile Association★. A radio device is hidden in one of 30 places within a car. When the car is reported stolen, the device is activated by remote control; it then transmits a signal which can be picked up by the police, who then attempt to recover your car. A number of patrol cars in most areas of the country carry Tracker detectors and there are others at various points around the M25 as well as at ports around the UK. Tracker can also be used in caravans, 2,000 of which are stolen each year.

Many car insurance companies offer a discount (usually around 10 per cent) for cars fitted with this system. However, it will not deter a thief from breaking into or taking the car because it is not obvious that the system has been fitted.

It remains to be seen whether the tracking system will become more widespread in use than it is at present.

Sold Secure Partnership Against Car Theft

A number of police authorities have recently joined together to try to ensure that no new or used car is sold without security devices. Contact Sold Secure PACT★ for more details.

Approved car security devices

With such a wide variety of products available, and such difficulty in making the correct judgement on effectiveness, the Association of British Insurers★ has developed an approval scheme for car security devices. At the moment this is restricted to alarms and electronic immobilisers, and it assumes that these have been professionally fitted.

The scheme is in its early days, and only a limited number of products has so far been tested and approved. But this number is likely to increase in the near future. Many car insurance companies will allow you a discount on your premium if you have an approved security device. To find out the latest details, send a large stamped addressed envelope to the Association of British Insurers★.

SENSIBLE PRECAUTIONS

- **Always lock your car and set any security devices** every time you leave it. The most common area left unlocked is the boot or rear hatch, the second most common the front passenger door.
- **Do not leave anything of value on view.** Around 60 per cent of theft from cars is opportunistic, so do not make your car more attractive or tempting to a thief.
- **Park in well-lit, busy areas.**
- **Fit secure audio equipment with security features**, preferably including a removable front panel.
- **Fit locking wheel nuts**, especially to alloy wheels (although normal steel wheels and tyres are stolen too).
- **Have all glass marked** with the vehicle registration number. Thieves are less likely to steal a car for 'ringing' if they have to replace the marked glass.
- **Never leave any documents** in the car. And anything with your name and address on it makes it easier for a thief to get duplicate documents.
- **Consider buying an extra security device.** Make sure it is as visible as possible to act as a deterrent to would-be thieves.

Choosing a safe car

Everyone wants to be safe in his or her car. But, until recently, car safety was not really a hot subject and seemed to be ignored by all but Volvo. But was it? While Volvo has certainly produced cars that are safer than the average, and capitalised on that aspect in its advertising, all car manufacturers have to meet certain minimum standards, and many have gone a long way past them. So how do you make sure you are buying the safest car for you and your family?

Which type of safety?

You can look at car safety in two different ways:

- how good the car will be at keeping you out of an accident in the first place – **primary safety**
- how well it will protect you if you do crash – **secondary safety**.

These are two very different aspects of safety, and a car which is good at one is not necessarily the best at the other. Over the years there have been many developments which should have reduced your risk of being involved in an accident. Wide, radial-ply tyres have vast reserves of grip. Front-wheel drive has made the handling of everyday cars more predictable. Anti-lock brakes prevent the car from skidding under braking. The list goes on. The trouble is, there is little evidence that these impressive developments have cut down on the *number* of accidents. Some drivers, it seems, merely drive faster to take advantage of the improvements in design and, worse still, have accidents at a higher speed than they may have done in a more mundane car.

The *Which?* car safety ratings

While it is certainly worth buying a car packed with as many primary safety characteristics as you can afford, it is likely to be more beneficial to aim for one offering secondary safety features. *Which?* has been testing cars for safety since the early 1980s and has now compiled data on over 250 popular models. The rating system is the only one in the world which gives information on the performance of a new car in the whole mix of accidents that it is likely to encounter on the road. A team of highly experienced accident investigators partially strips down a car to examine 50 critical areas – the steering wheel or side structure of the car, for example – which can kill or injure you in an accident. The design of each area is assessed against what is known about how the area kills or injures people, and what is the best design practice to avoid death and injury. Each area is awarded a numerical score that reflects how well it has been designed and how often that area is likely to be involved in different types of crashes. Good design, therefore, in an area which often causes death or serious injury scores highly, whereas good design in a less important area adds less to the final score. The numerical scores for each area are added together and are then adjusted to take account of the weight of the vehicle, because you are likely to be better off in a heavier car.

Key secondary safety features to look for

While there are many aspects of a car's design on which you cannot make a judgement – the stiffness of the body plays an important part in an accident, for example – you can at least make sure that a car contains some elementary features that will reduce the risk of injury to you or other occupants. Below are outlined the main factors that should form an important part of your buying decision.

Weight

The weight of a car has a straightforward effect on your safety – generally, the heavier the car, the less likely you are to be injured in it. The best superminis are only as safe as the average small family car, for example.

Steering wheel

With the wearing of seat-belts now compulsory for all front-seat occupants, the overall risk of serious injury has been reduced. Another problem, however, has arisen. In a frontal accident there is a real risk that the driver's head will hit the steering wheel, causing facial injuries, sometimes serious. An airbag fitted into the centre of the steering wheel addresses this problem. In an accident, the airbag inflates almost instantaneously to cushion your face from the hard parts of the steering wheel. This feature is reckoned to be very worth while, though the case for front passenger-side airbags is less clear-cut; these are *not* safe if a rearward-facing child restraint is fitted to the front seat.

Airbags are a very recent development in Europe, and you are unlikely to find a car built before 1993 with one. On other cars you should therefore look for a steering wheel hub and spokes that are covered with deep energy-absorbing material, free from hard spots. Bad steering wheels have metallic parts exposed, and/or the bolt in the centre (holding the wheel to the column) close to the surface of the wheel. A thin covering over a prominent bolt will do little to protect you in an accident.

Front seat-belts

Unless it is very old indeed, any car you buy, new or used, will have inertia-reel front seat-belts. These allow you to move around in normal circumstances, but they lock in place in a crash. In principle, they are not as safe as the 'static' belts, which hold you firmly all the time, but inertia-reel seat-belts have been accepted as the standard as they are more comfortable, adjust automatically to more or less the right position and, above all, are convenient – so are more likely to be used. If you have trouble getting comfortable wearing a belt you may find one of the many cars with adjustable upper mountings in the doors most suitable.

Two recent developments on seat-belts worth looking out for are **pre-tensioners** and **web locking**. A pre-tensioner is a device, usually attached to the buckle, which yanks the belt back or down at the time of the accident. This tightens it a little more and cuts down on your forward movement. A web lock grasps the belt at the door end to prevent more belt being pulled through the spooled-up webbing. It is difficult to spot either of these yourself on a car, but it is easy enough to check with a car dealer or the manufacturer/importer.

Rear seat-belts

While rear seat-belts have been fitted to new cars by law for some time, and it is now compulsory for rear-seat passengers to wear them, there are still many cars without rear belts. The importance of having them cannot be overemphasised. Not only does an unrestrained rear passenger run the risk of serious injury in an accident, but it is also bad news for those in the front seats, who can be severely injured by a rear passenger flying forward.

Even if a car does not have a full set of seat-belts, they are easy enough to install on most cars under 20 years old. Most have the mounting points already built in under the seat cushion and in the rear pillar.

Head restraints

In order to protect your neck in a rear impact, a head restraint needs to be strong, stable and high enough to support your whole head. You should check this on a car you are considering because there are still many cars around which do not provide enough adjustment for tall people. Remember, too, that those in the back seat are equally in need of protection, though finding cars with rear head restraints is not so easy.

Padding

The purpose of interior padding is to stop your head or other parts of your body hitting hard metal parts. It is very difficult to judge the quality of padding, so the best you can do is to make sure that the car you are considering does not have any exposed metal parts, especially bolts and hard fittings.

Other matters

There are many other aspects to secondary safety which are impossible for the lay person to judge. *Which?* appraisals are carried out by a team with many years of experience in investigating the causes of injuries in road accidents. Particular areas of concern are:

- the **strength of the seat**
- **hard objects** below the dashboard which could injure the driver's and front passenger's legs
- **door design**, particularly side impact beams and strong door catches
- **bodyshell strength**
- **well-protected fuel system and electrics**, to avoid the risk of fire.

There is still a way to go, however, before even the most modern cars incorporate the whole range of possible safety features.

Learning to drive more safely

The vast majority of people who pass their driving test take no further tuition, which means that they definitely have no tutored experience on motorways, and may well never have driven on dual carriageways, at night or in the rain.

There is much to be said for some additional post-test driving tuition, and it does not necessarily take much additional time or expense. Other than improving your driving standards, an additional safe-driving qualification can help reduce your insurance premiums.

Post-test training

The government has recently launched a new scheme – PASS PLUS – to encourage newly qualified drivers to take extra lessons after their driving test. PASS PLUS has been designed by the Driving Standards Agency* to improve skills in observation, hazard perception and awareness – factors known to make drivers safer but which can take years to acquire on the road. The scheme involves six training sessions with an Approved Driving Instructor (ADI), covering:

- town driving
- adverse weather conditions
- out-of-town and rural road driving
- night driving
- dual carriageways
- motorways.

The Driving Instructors Association (DIA)* offers something similar. Around a third of all approved driving instructors are members of the DIA, and any can offer a course of lessons after the test has been passed. Once you have completed the course to a satisfactory standard you will be eligible for an insurance discount through a specialist broker.

Advanced driving

The Institute of Advanced Motorists (IAM)* and the Royal Society for the Prevention of Accidents (ROSPA)* and other national driving schools such as BSM* promote safer driving by offering 'advanced driving tests'. You can get help and guidance from them about improving your driving standards as well as how to go about dealing with the test itself. All organisations are able to recommend insurance companies that offer preferential rates to those who have passed the test.

Carrying children in cars

Just as it is vital for adults to use seat-belts in cars, it is essential that children are strapped in too. Every year over 9,000 children under 11 years of age are killed or injured in car accidents. The big fear is that a child will be thrown right out of a car, which is more likely than you might think, and usually has very serious consequences.

It is impossible to support a child properly in your own arms, even if you are securely belted-in yourself. A child's effective weight can increase 20-fold in an accident, tearing the child free. It is equally dangerous to put one belt around both you and a child. Your weight could well crush the child. The only effective answer is to put a child into a proper child safety restraint every time. The law lays down the following rules:

Babies and children under 3   In the front seat a child restraint must *always* be worn. In the back seat a child restraint must be used if one is available. If one is not, then the law says that a restraint need not be used.

Children from 3 to 11   As long as the child is under 1.5m (5ft) tall, he or she *must* wear an appropriate child restraint if one is available. If not, then the child *must* wear an adult belt, even though this is not nearly as effective as a proper child seat.

Children 12 and above   Older children, and those over 1.5m (5ft) tall, *must* wear an adult belt if one is fitted, wherever they sit in the car.

Choosing a child restraint

All child safety restraints have to undergo a series of approval tests before they can be sold as such. Most manufacturers make their seats to the European Regulation ECE44 as this allows them to be sold throughout Europe. Seats made to these regulations will have a label marked with 'E' followed by a number, referring to the country where the seat was tested. You will probably see mention of ECE44 on the packaging too.

In addition, there are three British Standards for child restraints:

● BS AU 202a for rearward-facing seats
● BS3254 Part 2 for forward-facing seats and booster cushions
● BS AU 185 for booster cushions.

Seats and restraints to any of these standards are suitable for your child. The key factor in selecting the right type of seat is the child's weight rather than his or her age. All seats are held in place by the adult belt.

Stage 1
Weight limit 0 to 10kg (0 to 22lb)
Age range 0 to around 9 months
This is a rearward-facing baby seat which can be carried in the front or the back seat of the car – the back is preferable for the child's safety. These seats have built-in straps to hold the child in place.

Stage 1–2
Weight limit 0 to 18kg (0 to 40lb)
Age range 0 to around 4 years
This can be used as a rearward-facing baby seat until the child is old enough to sit up, and then converted into a forward-facing seat until the child is around four years old. Built-in straps hold the child in place.

Stage 2
Weight limit 9 to 18kg (20 to 40lb)
Age range around 6 months to 4 years
This is a forward-facing seat for children who can sit up. Built-in straps hold the child in place.

Stage 2–3
Weight limit 9 to 25kg (20 to 55lb)
Age range around 6 months to 6 years
Seats with a bigger age and weight range than Stage 2 seats.

Stage 3
Weight limit 15 to 36kg (33 to 80lb)
Age range around 4–11 years
These are booster cushions, which raise the child off the car seat so that the adult safety belt fits them properly.

It is immediately obvious from the above list of types of child seat that there is a good deal of overlap in age and weight. You have to decide whether you choose seats which cover a broad age range or those designed for a more particular size of child. *Which?* has tested all types for safety, and while there is every reason to believe that any child seat will provide a great deal of protection in an accident, some are better than others.

For the youngest children, buy a Stage 1 seat rather than a Stage 1–2. The former is generally safer and makes it easier to carry a sleeping baby around. Then move straight to a Stage 2–3 seat, where both the seat and the child are held in place with the adult belt. The trouble with Stage 2 seats, which are held in place with the adult belt and then the child is strapped into a separate harness within the seat, is that with inertia-reel seatbelts the seats move forward too much in an accident. Amazingly, European Regulation ECE44 still allows testing with obsolete static safety belts, which can fasten the seat much tighter. Stage 2–3 seats proved safer in *Which?* tests (August 1993) with the inertia-reel belts.

After that you may still need to buy a booster cushion (Stage 3) to improve the fit of an adult belt around your child. The diagonal section of the seat-belt should pass over the child's shoulder midway between the neck and the tip of the shoulder. The lap section should not ride up over the soft tummy area, but sit low on the thighs.

Whatever type of seat you decide to buy, you need to be sure that it is suitable for your particular car. If you cannot try it out before you buy, check that the shop will take it back if it proves to be unsuitable. When you put it in the car, check the following:

● the car's **seat-belt is long enough** – most likely to be a problem with rearward-facing or two-way seats

163

- the car's **seat-belt buckle does not rest on the frame** of the seat or interfere with it in any way
- the **seat-belt holds the child seat tightly** into the junction of the car seat back and cushion.

You should also never use a rearward-facing child seat opposite an airbag, though this is fine with forward-facing seats.

Fitting a child safety seat

It is essential that these seats are fitted correctly into place; otherwise their effectiveness in an accident is severely compromised. Yet despite the ease with which modern child safety equipment can be installed, many seats are not fitted correctly. You must follow the fitting instructions to the letter, the first time and on every other occasion that you place the seat in the car.

The majority of child seats are now held in place with the car's own adult seat-belt. Some seats then have their own built-in harness which restrains the child in place, while others make use of the adult belt once more. The intention with all these products is to avoid removing seat cushions, finding concealed mounting points and bolting in attachment straps – you just make use of a safety system which is already there. The other advantage is that it is straight-forward to move the seat from one car to another – as long as it is suitable for both models of car.

If you have a car without rear seat-belts it is still possible to buy child seats with their own fastening straps. Fitting is a bit more involved, but as long as you can wield a spanner the job is pretty straightforward. If you do not feel confident doing the job, most garages will do it for you for a small fee.

Street safety

It is difficult to open the newspapers or watch the television without hearing something about street crime. But the chances of your being a victim, particularly of violent street crime, are fairly small. Of all the crimes committed in the street, car crime is the one you're most likely to fall foul of. The 1993 British Crime Survey estimated that one in five car owners were victims of car-related crime in 1993. In contrast, the survey estimate of the risk of robbery or theft happening to you is just over one in a hundred. The risk of actual wounding as a result of an attack by a total stranger on the street is much smaller.

How likely you are to be a victim of some type of crime changes according to where you live. You are almost three and a half times more likely than the national average to be a victim of 'robbery or theft from the person' in the most crime-ridden inner cities. In rural areas the chance drops to half the national average.

Even though the risk of crime on the street is fairly small, you can still take sensible precautions, particularly if you live in an inner-city area. Follow the advice given below on how you can cut down the risk. Many of the safety points are directed at women in particular, but they can be useful for anyone who might feel vulnerable in certain street situations.

On the street

- **Bags and valuables**. Keep important possessions out of obvious sight. Cover up expensive-looking jewellery if you can and, if you carry a handbag, keep it close to your body or put it under your jacket or coat. Keep your cheque card separate from your cheque book and never carry your personal identification number (PIN).
- **Keys**. Keep keys in a pocket rather than in a bag. If your bag does get stolen, at least you'll still be able to get into your home and not have to worry about the attacker having your keys and your address. Never attach your name and address to your keys.
- **Walking**. If you are out walking on a lonely street or at night, walk facing the traffic and near the kerb with your bag on your side nearest the traffic. There will be less chance for an attacker to pull up behind you in a car or jump out from a doorway.
- **Jogging**. If you regularly go jogging or cycling, try to vary your route and time so that there is less chance of a prospective attacker knowing your routine.
- **Being followed**. If you think someone is following you, cross the road. If he follows you, cross again and keep moving quickly. Head for the nearest place where there will be people – a pub, for instance, or a house with lights on.
- **Travelling on public transport**. On buses at night sit near the driver or conductor. On a train if possible sit in a compartment

where there are several other people – even better if it is a compartment which will be near the exit at your destination.

- **Advice for men**. Be aware of how you might appear to a woman on her own. Try not to walk too closely behind a woman on a lonely street; instead, cross to the other side of the road. Don't sit too close to a woman on her own in a railway carriage.

In the car

- **Parking**. If you can, park in well-lit, busy areas, especially if you need to return to your car after dark. When you come back to your car, have your keys ready to open the door straight away. Check that no one is inside before you get in. In car parks, back into the space when you park so that you can drive away quickly.
- **Breaking down**. If you think your car is developing a fault and could break down, try to stop near a phone or where there are people about. If you frequently have to travel alone after dark, consider getting a mobile phone. If you do break down, don't accept lifts from strangers and, if you're on a motorway, walk to the nearest free emergency phone – you shouldn't have to walk more than half a kilometre (550 yards). If you have to stop on the hard shoulder, you're safer from traffic if you wait on the embankment rather than in the car. If you feel threatened, go back to the car, sit in the passenger side and lock yourself in.
- **Being followed**. If you think you are being followed by another car, drive to the nearest place with people – a garage, for instance. Don't stop and get out of the car unless there are other people around.
- **Being flagged down**. If someone flags you down on a quiet road, try to make sure it is a genuine emergency before you open a window or get out of the car.
- **Valuables**. Keep your doors locked and valuables away from windows, especially when driving slowly in towns.

Safety on holiday

In cities with a bad reputation for crime, tourists need to be extra wary.

- **Dress down**. In cities in poor countries especially, tourists displaying ostentatious wealth are obvious targets.
- **Leave as much money as possible in your hotel**, preferably in a safety-deposit box. You can use a moneybelt to keep the cash you need for the day, but keep some change in your pocket so that you don't have to dig into your moneybelt every time you want to buy a postcard.
- **Don't carry a shoulder bag** that can be easily grabbed.
- If you have a **day pack**, wear it on your front, where you can see it, rather than on your back. Thieves have been known to slash the bottoms of back packs without the wearer knowing about it.
- Try to look as if **you know where you're going**. In a city or in any area with a particularly bad reputation for street crime, it's worth studying a map and getting to know the layout of the place before you set out. Standing on street corners consulting a map makes you more vulnerable.
- Be especially on your guard at **busy bus and railway stations**. These are favourite haunts of pickpockets and bag snatchers.

Luggage

If you want to cut down on the risk of your luggage disappearing *en route*, follow this bag survival guide:

- Remove any **old airline baggage tags**.
- Ensure bags are **name-labelled**.
- Put your name, destination, airline and flight number on a **sticky label inside your bag**. This will help the airline trace you if your bag does go astray.
- **Lock your suitcase** if you can.
- Use tape to **make your bag distinctive**.
- **Check the bag** as soon as you take it off the carousel to make sure it's yours.

Money and valuables

- Always keep a record of **traveller's cheque numbers** and emergency contact details separate from the cheques.
- Use **hotel safety-deposit boxes** if available.

At the seaside

Holidays by the sea can have their extra dangers. When you first arrive, look out for information, warning signs and flags.

- **Check tide times**. If you move away from the main beach, make sure you're not going to get stranded by the tide.
- **Do not swim too near pipes, rocks, breakwaters and piers**. A large wave could knock you against them. Avoid swimming near windsurfers and other craft.
- Get out of the sea before you get too **cold**. The cold is probably the main cause of death by drowning in the UK: it can leave even strong swimmers unable to swim.
- **Don't swim on a full stomach** – you could get cramp. Swimming after too much alcohol can be lethal.
- **Don't dive** unless you are sure that the water is deep enough.
- It's **safer not to go swimming by yourself**. If you get into trouble, there may be no one around to help.
- If you get caught in a **strong tide** while you are swimming, don't swim against it. Swim sideways and out of its pull.

IF YOU ARE ATTACKED

- **Let go of your bag**. If someone tries to grab your bag, your instinctive reaction may be to hold on to it. Police advice, however, is to let it go. You could risk injury by resisting.
- **Stay calm**. If you are attacked, or are cornered by an attacker, you should try to stay calm while looking for a way of briefly surprising or delaying your attacker. Consider swearing or screaming loudly at your attacker, or you could set off a personal alarm. Basically, you need to think in terms of anything that may catch your attacker off guard so that you can run away.
- **Use self-defence**. Self-defence techniques may give you a few vital seconds in which to get away. You can find out about courses from your local library or police station.
- **Use a weapon**. An object that you might normally carry with you, such as keys, a spray or an umbrella, can be used as a weapon in self-defence and may help you get away.

CHAPTER 4

INSURANCE

HOWEVER careful you are, and whatever precautions you take, you can never guard yourself completely against life's perils. But you can protect yourself from the financial consequences of unforeseen disasters by taking out appropriate insurance.

In this chapter, we look at various types of insurance to cover your home, your possessions, your safety at home and away, and your legal rights.

House buildings insurance

Buying your own home is likely to be one of the biggest financial commitments you'll ever make. If you take out a mortgage, as most people do, the mortgage lender will insist that the home is adequately insured. Even if you own your home outright, you would be unwise not to insure it.

What's covered?

House buildings insurance pays out if you suffer loss or damage to your home because of any of the 'insured perils' – see Box overleaf. A typical buildings policy covers the following items:

- **rebuilding** your home (including garages, outbuildings, fences, swimming-pools, and so on) if it is completely destroyed
- **repairs** to your home if it is damaged
- **alternative accommodation** if you can't live in your home while rebuilding or repairs are being carried out
- **underground pipes and cables** serving your home
- **windows** and other fixed glass
- **toilets, baths and other fixed sanitary ware.**

Buildings insurance also covers your legal liability as owner of the home. Suppose, say, a slate fell from your roof and badly injured a passer-by. You could face a huge claim from that person and you simply might not have the money to meet it. But the legal liability section of your policy would pay out.

HOUSE INSURANCE – THE INSURED PERILS

Most house buildings and contents policies will pay out if the injury, loss or damage for which you're claiming was caused by any of the following perils:

- fire, explosion, lightning or earthquake
- storms and floods (though cover for fences and gates might be excluded)
- subsidence, heave or landslip
- falling trees
- theft or attempted theft
- riots, vandals and political disturbances
- bursting, leaking or overflowing of pipes, water tanks, washing machines and so on
- breaking or collapsing TV and radio aerials
- vehicles or animals crashing into your property
- impact by aircraft or things falling from them
- leakage of oil

How much cover?

If you choose a conventional house buildings policy, you decide how much cover you need and you are charged a given premium rate for each £1,000 of cover. These policies work on the basis that the sum insured is the cost of rebuilding your home if it was completely destroyed. It is vital that you don't insure for less than this amount, because any claim – even for just a small sum – could then be scaled down in proportion to the amount by which you're under-insured.

The rebuilding cost of your home is not the same as its market price. Rebuilding cost is based on the cost of clearing the debris of your destroyed home from the site and then rebuilding with the same types of material. Surprisingly, the result of this calculation will often come to more than the market price of your home – even though the market price reflects not just the value of the home but also the land it stands on.

The Association of British Insurers★ publishes a guide to the rebuilding cost of different homes, depending on the type of home, its age, size and whereabouts in the country it's located.

The alternative to conventional policies are bedroom-rated policies – see page 173. With these, a set maximum level of cover and an associated premium are dictated partly by the number of bedrooms your home has. Even if you choose this type of policy, you should still work out the rebuilding cost of your home in order to check that the cover on offer matches your needs.

Most policies automatically index-link the amount of cover you have by increasing it in line with the House Rebuildings Cost Index. If yours does not, you'll need to take account of inflation each time you renew your policy.

House contents insurance

The Association of British Insurers★ estimates that around a quarter of people don't have house contents insurance. If you're one of them, it's not just the possessions in your home that are at risk. A contents policy is also a catch-all for some other important types of protection.

What's covered?

House contents insurance covers the contents of your home – such as your clothes, furniture, TV – against loss or damage due to any of the 'insured perils' – see Box on previous page. In addition, it will usually cover:

- **your possessions against the 'insured perils'** while they are temporarily out of the home – such as things you take on holiday with you – though the theft cover might be reduced
- **accidental damage** to television sets, video recorders, hi-fis, mirrors and glass in furniture
- if you're a tenant, **damage to your landlord's buildings**, decoration, furniture, and so on

- **replacement keys** if these are lost or stolen
- the cost of **alternative accommodation** if, say, a break-in or flood leaves your home uninhabitable for a time
- **your legal liability to other people** if you accidentally injure them or damage their property. This cover is not restricted to accidents that happen at home, so it gives you an important general protection if, say, you accidentally tripped up a man in the street with the result that he broke his ankle and an expensive camera he was carrying
- some policies give cover for **money, credit cards**, and so on
- often there is a sum payable on the **death of you or your husband or wife** in specified circumstances, such as a house fire. The amount is very small and no substitute for adequate life insurance.

Optional extras

With the exception of a few items like TVs, standard contents insurance does not cover your possessions if they are damaged by accident – such as by spilling paint on the carpet, or the kids breaking a table being used as part of a game. You can usually add 'accidental damage' cover for an extra premium.

A more comprehensive extension to a standard policy is 'all risks' cover. This covers some or all of your possessions (you choose which) against any perils – not just those on the 'insured perils' list – unless they are specifically excluded (see page 174). Generally, all risks cover gives this protection even if your property is away from home. But if you take items outside the UK, cover is generally limited to a period of 30 or 60 days. The all risks section may extend to items such as money, credit cards, travel tickets, jewellery, and so on, which are often not included in a standard policy.

Other types of cover which are often optional extras, rather than part of a standard policy, include:

- the cost of **replacing food** if your freezer stops working – e.g. because of a power cut
- cover for **caravans and boats**
- payment of **legal expenses** (solicitor's and barrister's fees, court fees etc.) you incur if you sue someone who has injured you or damaged your property

- **personal accident cover**, which pays out small amounts in certain specified situations – e.g. you lose your sight.

How much cover?

The majority of contents policies give you 'new-for-old' cover for most of your possessions. This means there is no reduction for wear and tear, so the amount paid out would be enough to replace the lost or damaged items with brand new ones. But 'indemnity cover' – where a reduction is made for wear and tear – typically applies to clothing and linen.

To work out how much to insure for, you need to calculate the replacement cost of every item in your home, using current shop prices for the articles covered on a new-for-old basis and secondhand prices for anything covered on an indemnity basis.

Contents policies require you to insure for the replacement of all your possessions. If you insure for less than the full amount, any claims could be scaled down to reflect the amount by which you're under-insured.

Even if you choose a bedroom-rated policy (where a set maximum amount of cover and associated premium are based partly on the number of bedrooms your home has), you should still calculate the replacement cost of your possessions to check whether the cover on offer matches your needs.

Many policies automatically index-link the amount of cover you have. If yours does not, you'll need to increase your new-for-old cover to take account of inflation each time you renew the policy. Don't forget to alter the level of cover when you buy new things or get rid of possessions.

What house insurance does not cover

It's important to realise that no insurance policy covers absolutely everything that could go wrong. Both buildings insurance and contents insurance pay out only if the loss or damage occurs because of one of the perils listed in the policy. If what happens to your home or possessions is not listed, the chances are that there is no cover for that eventuality. On top of that, certain perils are specifically excluded. These include war, radioactive contamination and damage caused by sonic bangs.

The policy is also likely to spell out a number of other exclusions, for example:

- damage due simply to **normal wear and tear**
- injury, damage or loss which occurs because **you haven't maintained your home** or possessions properly
- damage due to **gradually operating causes**, such as rot, mildew or woodworm
- any **'compulsory excess'** – i.e. the first part of a claim which you're required to pay yourself. Such excesses are common, for example, with subsidence cover
- injury, damage or loss which is connected to **your running a business from home**
- certain claims – e.g. due to theft or burst pipes – if the **home is left unoccupied or unfurnished** for more than a given period – usually 30 days
- **legal liability** won't usually cover claims by members of your own family or by people you employ in your home
- if you're in the process of selling your home, buildings cover usually stops on **completion of the sale**.

In addition, limits might apply to certain sections of the policy. For example, legal liability cover might be restricted to a maximum of £500,000, alternative accommodation to 20 per cent of the total sum you're insured for, and contents policies may set an upper limit on the 'deemed value' of any individual item.

Restrictions might apply to particular types of property. For example, bicycle theft is so common that there is often no theft cover unless a bicycle is securely locked.

'Consequential loss' is also excluded. This means, for example, that while the cost of replacing stolen car keys is covered, there would be no cover for replacing a car steering lock that couldn't be unlocked because the keys had been stolen.

You are expected to take sensible precautions to prevent injury, loss or damage. For example, a theft claim would be turned down if it was discovered that you'd nipped out for a few minutes leaving the outside doors unlocked.

How much does house insurance cost?

Cost will depend to a large part on where you live. In general, you'll pay more in a city than a rural area because crime-related claims tend to be much higher in urban areas. Burglaries triggered 834,000 claims (average £890) against house contents insurance in 1993 and are also a major reason for buildings insurance claims.

TOP FIVE CAUSES OF HOUSE INSURANCE CLAIMS

Buildings insurance: storm damage, accidental damage, burglary, burst/leaking pipes, rain/flood damage
Contents insurance: burglary, accidental damage, water damage, accidental loss, fire/smoke damage

Most commonly claimed items
Roof tile, jewellery, carpets, windows/glass, electrical equipment, camera/lenses, video recorders/camcorders, interior decorations, clothing, clocks/watches

---

Some areas of the country – particularly the South-East – have had more problems than others with subsidence. Residents there can expect to pay more for their buildings insurance. The type of home you live in will also influence the amount you pay for buildings cover which costs more if, for example, your home is built of unusual materials (making it expensive to rebuild) or has a thatched roof (more at risk from fire).

There are, however, steps you can take to keep down the cost of cover:

● **check the level of cover**. You should avoid being under-insured, but don't pay for more cover than you need. Check that index-linked policies are still in line with the value of your property and possessions. If you have a bedroom-rated policy, check that it's not over the top for your needs

● **make your home more secure**. If you live in an area with a high risk of theft, your insurance company might insist that you

install special door and window locks, security bolts and even a burglar alarm. If not, you might be able to get a discount of, say, 5 or 10 per cent if you voluntarily fit the devices. Joining a Neighbourhood Watch scheme might also earn a discount
● **agree to a 'voluntary excess'**. This means that you volunteer to pay the first part of any claim yourself. Depending on the size of the excess, the discount could range from 5 to 20 per cent, say. Bear in mind, though, that a voluntary excess is in addition to any compulsory excesses which apply
● **shop around**. Premiums vary widely from company to company. Moreover, some policies offer special discounts if, say, you have a particular occupation or are aged over 50. No claims discounts, which are more common with car insurance (see later in the chapter), are also available on some house contents policies. For more about shopping for insurance, see pages 187–8.

If you take out a mortgage to buy your home, the lender will probably try to persuade you to buy house buildings insurance through that company – and possibly contents insurance too. Taking up the policies offered might be part and parcel of a special mortgage package, but, if it's not, you don't have to buy through this route and you may well find a cheaper deal elsewhere. Building societies sometimes charge an 'administration fee' (say, £25 to £30) if you choose your own buildings insurance, but shopping around can sometimes save you this much and more, so don't be deterred.

Car insurance

By law, you must have some insurance cover before you can drive a car on a public road.

What's covered?

The legal minimum is a third party insurance. This covers any injury you cause to your passengers or anyone else and any damage you cause to other people's cars and other property.

Given that there were 326,500 claims for theft either of a car or from a car in 1993, it's not surprising that the legal minimum is generally considered to be inadequate. Most people choose either:

- **a third party, fire and theft policy**. This adds cover for theft and attempted theft of the car and for damage to the car caused by fire, lightning or explosion. There is usually a compulsory excess of, say, £100; *or*
- **a comprehensive policy**. In addition to third party, fire and theft cover, this also covers accidental damage to your own car. There may be a compulsory excess on this part of the policy, especially when young or inexperienced drivers are driving. Comprehensive policies also provide other benefits, typically: cover for theft of hi-fis and other possessions from the car, limited medical expenses, and cash sums if you or your husband or wife are severely injured. Some policies pay for a hire car to replace yours while it's off the road following an accident.

Your policy will cover you fully for using your car in the UK and give you the legal minimum cover (usually just third party) elsewhere in the European Union (EU). If you intend to drive abroad, you should extend your insurance to cover you fully outside the UK. You do this by getting a 'green card' from your insurance company – some companies make a charge, with others it's free.

Whatever type of policy you have, the insurance company or your broker will often be able to add on legal expenses insurance (see pages 186–7).

As with all insurance, some risks won't be covered. Check your policy carefully.

How much does it cost?

Cost depends on a variety of factors:

- **type of cover**. Comprehensive costs significantly more than third party, fire and theft
- **your car**. Insurance companies sort cars into 20 groups according to how expensive they are to repair and replace, their performance and claims experience
- **where your car is kept**. Living in a city or high crime area could treble your premium. Crime statistics show that your car is 50 times more likely to be stolen if you park on the road rather than in a garage
- **who's insured**. Statistics show that mature drivers make fewer

claims than younger ones, so the over-50s or 60s qualify for discounts with some companies. Young drivers tend to be high risks and pay substantially more for insurance. If a young son or daughter is to be included on your policy, as well as an extra premium, there may be a hefty compulsory excess when they are at the wheel. Your occupation may also affect your premium – for instance, entertainers, journalists and sportspeople often pay more

- **driving record**. If you have a record of accidents, claims and/or driving offences, expect to pay a higher premium. You might even be refused insurance. (Convictions are deemed to be 'spent' after five years and can't then be taken into account by the insurance company)

- **how the car is used**. Most private car policies do not cover you for driving your car on business (other than getting to and from work). If you need business cover, you may have to pay extra.

Ways to keep the cost down

Most policies offer a substantial no claims discount (NCD) on your premium if you don't make any claims. The more years without a claim, the larger the discount. The Table shows a typical discount scale, but some companies offer maximum discounts of 65 or even 70 per cent.

Before making a claim, you need to weigh up whether the amount you'll get is more than the NCD you'll lose. If it's not, then it would not be worth making a claim.

By paying extra for your insurance, you can protect your NCD. For an extra 15 per cent, say, a protected NCD policy might let you make two claims in any five-year period without losing any NCD. For 20 per cent extra, you might be able to make any number of claims. But note that if you make a lot of claims the insurance company might increase your basic premium (reflecting the fact that you're a bad risk) even though your NCD is unchanged.

Typical no claims discount

	Number of years since policy started or last claim made					
	1	2	3	4	5	6
Typical discount scale	30%	40%	50%	60%	60%	60%
Discount at renewal if you have a 60% NCD and make a claim	40%	50%	60%	60%	60%	60%
Discount at renewal if you have a 50% NCD and make a claim	30%	40%	50%	60%	60%	60%
Discount at renewal if you have a 40% NCD and make a claim	0%	30%	40%	50%	60%	60%
Discount at renewal if you have a 30% NCD and make a claim	0%	0%	30%	40%	50%	60%

You can transfer your NCD from one company to another if you switch insurer. If you haven't had car insurance before but have been driving (e.g. on your spouse's or parent's policy), you may qualify for a starter discount of, say, 25 per cent.

Another way to keep down the cost of car insurance is to agree to a voluntary excess (see page 176). If you would not make small claims anyway because of the effect on your NCD, it makes sense to choose an excess of at least that amount. Bear in mind that the voluntary excess is on top of any compulsory excesses which apply to your policy.

An increasing number of companies will give you a discount if you fit approved security devices to your car to reduce the likelihood of theft. Discounts range from 2.5 to 20 per cent.

Ask your insurance company or broker what discounts are available. For tips on shopping for car insurance, see pages 187–8.

Holiday insurance

There's some overlap between holiday insurance, house contents insurance and health services available to UK citizens – so much so that, if you're holidaying in the UK, you might not need holiday insurance at all (though the cancellation cover could be useful).

But, if you're holidaying abroad, the picture is different. Around one person in fifteen who takes out holiday insurance makes a claim – half for cancellation, a quarter for medical bills and most of the rest for lost or stolen baggage. So don't leave home without it.

What's covered?

The type and amount of cover vary, so make sure you get a copy of the policy document and check that the cover is sufficient before you buy. You may need to be persistent about this, because tour operators – who often sell their own cover along with holiday packages – all too frequently don't have the policy to hand.

If the cover offered by a tour operator is inadequate, buy your insurance elsewhere. You're not obliged to accept the operator's cover, but some operators do make price discounts dependant on your taking out their insurance (on which they earn commission).

Here we set out the cover which you ideally need:

- **medical expenses** to cover the cost of treating you or any of your party if you're taken ill. It also covers the cost of flying the patient home in an emergency. You need a minimum £250,000 cover for Europe and £1 million for anywhere else in the world Don't skimp on this cover, even if you're going to another EU country and have a form E111 (see Box). If you have private medical insurance (see pages 184–6), it might cover you while you're abroad
- **cancellation or curtailment** refunds what you've paid for the holiday if you can't go after all, for example, because of illness, death, being called up for jury service or being made redundant – check precisely what your policy covers. Good policies also cover extra costs (e.g. for more expensive flights) if you have to come home early. It's essential that you arrange this cover either before or at the time you book your holiday
- **personal liability** provides cover – including legal costs – if anyone claims against you for injury or damage that you've caused. Ideally, you need £2 million cover for the USA and £1 million for elsewhere in the world. You'll probably have similar cover

under your house contents insurance – this is likely to be adequate if you're holidaying in the UK, but check whether cover extends abroad and whether the amount is sufficient

● **baggage** – it is surprising how the value of the things you pack in your suitcase mounts up. Cover of £1,500 would not be too much for most people. If you have all risks house contents insurance (see earlier in the chapter), you may already have cover for your baggage – for a UK holiday anyway – but check carefully where the cover is valid, how long it lasts and the amount before deciding to go without holiday insurance

● **money and documents**. Usually these are covered only up to a fairly low limit – e.g. £500 for money. Check precisely what cover is provided for travellers' cheques, airline tickets, replacement passports and so on.

If you're sure you already have enough protection through some other type of insurance, see if you can get a discount on your holiday insurance by removing or reducing the duplicate cover.

FREE MEDICAL TREATMENT IN EUROPE

The UK has reciprocal arrangements with other EU countries (and some other countries, such as Australia) which mean that you can get free emergency treatment if you're taken ill.

If you're visiting an EU country, get a form E111 through your post office and carry it with you while you're away. Don't view an E111 as a substitute for the medical cover provided by holiday insurance. The E111 entitles you only to emergency treatment. It doesn't cover painful but non-urgent conditions or the cost of flying you home if suitable treatment isn't available locally.

Exclusions

Read the exclusions carefully. Most policies do not cover:

● the **first part** of any claim – e.g. £25 – per person
● loss or theft **if you fail to report it** to the police within 24 hours
● claims arising from a **pre-existing medical condition** unless you told the insurance company about it and they agreed to cover you

- if you're travelling **against medical advice**
- medical claims if you're **over 32 weeks pregnant**
- claims arising from AIDS or HIV
- if you're **drunk or under the influence of drugs**
- if you **don't take reasonable care**. For example, a claim might be refused or reduced if you left belongings in a car overnight or unattended on a beach while you took a swim
- **fragile objects**. In addition, some policies don't cover contact lenses, hearing aids or dentures.

Many policies also exclude hazardous activities, such as ski-ing, climbing, parascending and so on. You would need to arrange extra cover for these.

How much does it cost?

Cost depends largely on whereabouts in the world you're travelling and the length of your stay. Cover for the UK is cheapest. Often it's most expensive for the USA.

Usually, you take out a policy just for a specific trip. But, if you take holidays several times a year, you may save by taking out year-long cover.

Cover for children under two is usually free.

Sickness and accident insurance

This type of insurance which pays out a lump sum or regular income if you suffer death, certain injuries or cannot work because of illness is usually fairly cheap and may seem a good idea on the face of it. But the pay-outs are low and may well duplicate benefits you can claim either from the state or your employer (see Box). If you do need this type of cover, consider instead the more expensive (but more comprehensive) benefits offered by life insurance (to provide a lump sum or income for your dependants if you die) or permanent health insurance (to replace lost income if you can't work because of illness or disability). These insurances are outside the scope of this book.

Accident insurance tailored to your particular risks may be useful if you participate in dangerous sports, such as climbing or shooting.

HELP FROM THE STATE AND YOUR EMPLOYER

If you're an employee, you may qualify for statutory sick pay (SSP) – paid by your employer – if you're off work because of health problems. SSP gives you a weekly sum (at one of two rates depending on your earnings) for a maximum of 28 weeks. Your employer may run a more generous sick pay scheme than the statutory minimum.

If you're self-employed, or an employee who either doesn't qualify for SSP or has been ill for more than 28 weeks, you may qualify for incapacity benefit. This can continue for as long as you are too ill or disabled to work or until you start to get state pension instead.

For details about state benefits, contact your local Benefits Agency.

What's covered?

Typically, the accident part of a policy will pay out a lump sum if an accidental injury results in your death, the loss of one or both arms, legs or eyes or your total disablement. If as a result of the accident you can't work, you'll also get a set weekly sum for up to two years, say – a reduced amount is payable if you can manage to work part-time. There may also be small payments towards medical costs or for each day you have to spend in hospital.

If the policy also includes a sickness section, this will generally pay out a set amount (worked out on a daily rate) if you're off work because of illness. The benefit typically lasts for a maximum of one year.

Check the policy carefully to see what's not covered. For example, some policies restrict cover to while you're in your car or at home – 24-hour cover is obviously much better.

How much does it cost?

Premiums depend on your work and how risky it's perceived to be, your age and sex (women are often charged more because they tend to have more days off work sick), your state of health, what hazardous activities you indulge in and how soon after an accident or onset of illness you want the policy to start paying out.

Medical expenses insurance

If you're injured or suddenly taken ill, the National Health Service (NHS) is likely to provide prompt and excellent treatment. But, if you have a non-urgent condition – a hernia, varicose veins or hip problem, say – you're likely to find yourself on a long waiting list. Avoiding delay is one reason why people turn to private treatment. Other reasons are treatment at a convenient time, having some choice over the specialists you see, and enjoying a private room and hotel-style facilities (TV, own bathroom etc).

But private treatment can cost an arm and a leg – and, because you don't know in advance when you might need treatment and how the costs might build up, it's hard to plan for. Private medical insurance (PMI) overcomes those difficulties – you pay the premiums and the insurance pays out when you need treatment. Some people have PMI cover as a perk through their job.

TYPICAL COST OF PRIVATE TREATMENT IN 1992

Hysterectomy	£3,300
Hip replacement	£5,300
Cataract removal	£2,000
Hernia	£1,400

Source: BUPA

What's covered?

PMI comes in several forms:

- **comprehensive policies**. These cover the full cost of eligible treatment, both as inpatient and outpatient. You may be covered while you're abroad as well as in the UK
- **standard policies**. Treatment as an inpatient is usually fully covered, though some plans put a limit on the amount they'll pay towards specialists' and anaesthetists' fees. A few plans fully cover

outpatient treatment but more often there are limits, especially on physiotherapy

● **budget plans**. There may be a cash limit on the claims you can make in any year. A popular variant is the six-week waiting plan, which pays for private treatment only if the NHS waiting list for the treatment you need is longer than six weeks. Most plans completely exclude outpatient cover unless it is related to a spell as an inpatient.

With all types of policy, hospitals are usually divided into three categories according to how expensive they are – limiting your choice to a lower category reduces your premiums. Some budget plans further limit your choice of hospital.

Exclusions

No policy covers all medical conditions. Common exclusions are long-term illnesses, such as multiple sclerosis, pregnancy, psychiatric problems, cosmetic surgery, and AIDS and HIV. Medical problems you have at the time you take out PMI may not be covered. Either they are 'underwritten' which means that you pay a higher premium or they are excluded completely, or they are covered after a waiting period of two years, provided the problem hasn't recurred during that time.

How much does it cost?

Comprehensive policies are the most costly. You can cut the cost by around a quarter if you settle for a standard plan. Budget plans can cost just a third of the price of comprehensive plans, but make sure the cover is still adequate.

Choosing a more restricted list of hospitals keeps down the cost but make sure that at least one of the listed hospitals is near you.

Cost also varies greatly with your age, since the likelihood of making a claim increases as you get older. However, plans for people aged over 60 qualify for basic-rate tax relief (even if you're a reduced rate or non-taxpayer).

A few companies offer reduced premiums in return for a voluntary excess (see page 176) ranging from, say £100 up to £500. One or two companies give a discount on PMI premiums if you also take out critical illness insurance (which pays out a lump sum if you're diagnosed with specified life-threatening conditions) and/or permanent health insurance.

Discounts are widely available if you have a particular occupation (e.g. teaching), or you belong to a certain professional body or organisation (e.g. the RAC). Ask the company or your broker for details.

Alternatives to PMI

If PMI is too costly for you, you could consider a **hospital cash plan**. This does not cover the cost of treatment, but pays out a fixed cash sum for every day you spend in hospital having either NHS or private treatment. You can use the money in any way you wish, including as a contribution towards the costs of 'going private'.

Another alternative to PMI is an **operation cost benefit policy**. This is more limited than PMI, covering say a dozen of the most common surgical treatments only. Some policies cover the full cost of the treatment. Others pay out a given sum depending on the type of operation.

Legal expenses insurance

Many people fail to pursue their legal rights because of the daunting costs of taking a case to court. Legal expenses insurance aims to remove this obstacle.

What's covered?

Legal expenses – i.e. the cost of solicitors, court fees, barrister's fees, and so on – are covered, usually up to a set maximum, if you sue somebody or somebody else sues you. You might also be covered for certain criminal proceedings and possibly cases brought before employment tribunals. The type of situations covered are:

- **personal injury cases**
- **loss or damage to property**
- **disputes over contracts** – e.g. with workmen, with a landlord or tenant, over the purchase or sale of your home

- **disputes with neighbours**
- **unfair dismissal claims** and certain other work-related disputes
- **consumer problems** – e.g. over defective goods or shoddy services
- **motoring offences.**

Usually, you will be covered for events which took place before you took out the policy provided you couldn't have known that a dispute was likely to arise out of them.

Exclusions

Routine legal work, such as house conveyancing, divorce, making a will and getting probate, is usually excluded, as are building work disputes.

If your expenses are covered by some other policy – e.g. your house or car insurance – you'll have to claim against the other policy, not the legal expenses insurance.

How much does it cost?

Stand-alone legal expenses insurance policies are relatively costly. However, policies added on to house insurance or, more commonly, car insurance are usually good value for money. They cover a limited range of disputes – for example, when attached to car insurance it will typically cover claiming your 'uninsured losses' (e.g. damage to your own car if you don't have comprehensive cover, a policy excess, lost NCD) if someone else is to blame for an accident in which you were injured or your car damaged.

Buying insurance

If you know which company you want to buy from, obviously you can contact the company direct. Regular surveys in *Which?* magazine and elsewhere can guide you to the best buys. However, very often your precise insurance needs and the cost of cover depend on personal factors, so published surveys – although a good starting point – are not enough. You should seek help in finding the best policy for you.

Only insurance intermediaries who are registered with the Insurance Brokers Registration Council (IBRC)* are allowed to call themselves 'brokers'. They must abide by a code of conduct and are committed to giving you independent advice. For a list of members in your area, contact the IBRC.

Other intermediaries for the types of insurance covered in this chapter go by a variety of names, such as 'agent' or 'consultant'. They are covered by a less rigorous code operated by the Association of British Insurers* through its member insurance companies.

The markets for car insurance and house insurance are especially competitive since the establishment of the so-called 'direct insurers'. They don't operate through brokers or other intermediaries – you phone them direct – and they usually use sophisticated computer programs to calculate the risk of insuring you and the premium they will charge. If you're a standard or low risk to insure, you will probably get a very good quote from these companies. If you're a poor risk, you might be charged a lot or refused cover altogether – in your case, a broker or other intermediary may be able to find you a better deal.

CHAPTER 5

FIRST AID

IN THE home accidents 'league table' the most common accident by far is falls, typically down stairs or steps. These account for 39 per cent of all non-fatal home accidents. Second, at 18 per cent, are accidents in which a person is hit by a dropped or moving object. Third, at 17 per cent, come cutting or piercing injuries, typically cased by knives, chisels or scissors.

Although home accidents are far more likely to be fairly minor mishaps than dangerous emergencies, whatever the injury, knowing and applying the basics of first aid can make a real difference. Follow this guide for the correct way to deal with some of the more serious household injuries that you may encounter.

In any accident it is important to ensure that it is safe for you to approach the injured person. For example, the person could still be holding a live electric cable. If it is safe to approach, check the response of the person by gently shaking him or her and shouting. If there is no response, follow the ABC of resuscitation.

Dealing with an unconscious casualty

The ABC of resuscitation

For anyone who is unconscious, you must:

1. Open the **Airway** – remove any obvious debris from the casualty's mouth, tilt the head back and lift the chin upwards (see illustration).
2. Check the **Breathing** – do this by looking, listening and feeling for breath for five seconds.
3. Check the **Circulation** – check the pulse in the casualty's neck for five seconds.

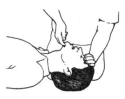

If breathing and pulse are present, place the casualty in the recovery position (see below).

If there is no breathing but a pulse is present, start **artificial ventilation**.

- Pinch the casualty's nose firmly.
- Take a deep breath and seal your lips around the casualty's lips.
- Blow slowly into the mouth, watching the chest rise and fall completely; give breaths at the rate of about 10 per minute.
- If you are on your own, give 10 breaths first, go to phone for an ambulance, then return quickly. Re-check the ABC procedure and continue as appropriate.
- Check for a pulse after every 10 breaths.
- When breathing restarts, place the casualty in the recovery position (see below).

If there is no breathing and no pulse, ring for an ambulance (or get someone else to do it). Re-check the ABC procedure, then give two breaths of artificial ventilation, before starting **chest compression**:

- Place the heel of the hand two fingers' breadth above the junction of the ribcage and breastbone.
- Place the other hand on top and interlock the fingers.
- Keeping the arms straight, press the chest down 4–5cm (1½–2in) 15 times, at a rate of about 80 per minute.

Repeat the cycle until the condition improves or medical help takes over. If the condition improves, re-check the pulse. If it is present, continue with artificial ventilation only if there is no spontaneous breathing.

The recovery position

Anyone who is breathing but unconscious with the heart beating should be placed in the recovery position, as follows:

- Turn the casualty on to his or her side, with the arm and leg on the ground at right angles to the body, and the head resting on the other hand. This keeps the person in a stable position.

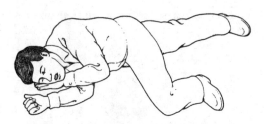

- Keep the head tilted back with the jaw forward.
- Make sure the person cannot roll over.
- Check the breathing and the pulse regularly.

Choking

- Slap the victim sharply between the shoulder blades up to five time. If this fails to dislodge the blockage, use the abdominal thrust technique: stand behind the choking person, put your arms around his or her waist and clasp your hands together in front above the navel. Give a sharp pull diagonally downwards. This must be strong enough to force air from the lungs to expel the blockage.
- Bend a baby or small child over your lap, and slap the back sharply between the shoulder blades. Do not use the abdominal thrust on children under one year old.

Drowning

- Follow the ABC of resuscitation (see page 189).
- Anyone rescued from drowning should be taken to hospital.

Bleeding

Serious bleeding needs to be dealt with straight away before the person is taken to hospital.

- Don't try to remove any embedded object.
- Apply pressure directly to the bleeding part with a clean pad or even your clean hand.
- If possible, raise the injured limb above the casualty's head.
- Apply a dressing of clean material and bandage firmly but not too tightly to staunch the bleeding. Don't remove it: if blood starts seeping through, apply another dressing on top.

Burns and scalds

- Do not remove any clothing.
- Quickly pour cold water over the injury or run it under a cold tap or shower for at least 10 minutes – this should soothe the pain and prevent deeper tissue damage.
- When the pain has subsided, wrap the burn or scald with a non-fluffy material such as a clean sheet. Cling-film can be effectively used to cover a burn – it peels off easily and painlessly.
- Don't give the person anything to eat or drink if you think medical treatment may be necessary.
- Don't use any creams or ointments.

Chemical burns

- If the eyes are involved (for example, if the eyes have been splashed by bleach or a similar product), treat them first by holding them open under a tap or shower for at least 10 minutes. Alternatively, pour jugs of clean water over them. Cover with a clean, non-fluffy dressing.
- Treat skin burns in a similar way.

Electric shock

- Switch off the current. If you can't, stand on dry, insulated material, such as a pile of newspapers or a rubber mat, and pull the person away from the source of the current without touching his or her skin – use something like a broom handle or a wooden chair.
- Follow the ABC of resuscitation if breathing has stopped (see page 189).
- Flood any burns with cold water, then cover them with a clean, non-fluffy dressing.
- Anyone who has had an electric shock should be taken to hospital.

Poisoning

- If the casualty is conscious, ask what happened in case he or she becomes unconscious.
- Do not make the person vomit. If he or she has already vomited, collect a sample to give to the hospital staff.
- If the lips are burning, give sips of milk or water.
- Place the person in the recovery position (see page 190).
- Get the person to hospital.

Broken bones

- In serious falls in which there may be a back, neck or skull injury, advise the person to stay still, and support the head at all times; place rolled-up blankets either side of the person's body. Keep him or her warm and wait for the ambulance crew to arrive.
- Support a broken limb above and below the injury with rolled-up blankets or towels so that it is immobilised.

Further information

These hints are no substitute for a thorough knowledge of first aid. St John Ambulance*, the British Red Cross Society* and St Andrew's Ambulance Association* hold courses throughout the UK. The information in this chapter was checked by St John Ambulance.

Addresses

Arthritis Care
18 Stephenson Way,
London NW1 2HD
Linkline 0800 289170
(12-4, Mon-Fri)
0171-916 1500 (10-4, Mon-Fri)

The Association of British Insurers
51 Gresham Street,
London EC2V 7HQ
0171-600 3333

Automobile Association
(for information about Tracker,
telephone your local shop –
number in *Yellow Pages*)

British Red Cross
National Headquarters,
9 Grosvenor Crescent,
London SW1X 7EJ
0171-235 5454

British Security Industry
Association (BSIA)
Security House, Barbourne Road,
Worcester WR1 1RS
01905 21464

Council for Registered Gas
Installers (CORGI)
4 Elmwood,
Chineham Business Park,
Crockford Lane,
Basingstoke RG24 8WG
01256 707060

Disabled Living Foundation
380-384 Harrow Road,
London W9 2HU
(please write only)

Driving Instructors Association
Safety House,
Beddington Farm Road,
Croydon CR0 4XZ
0181-665 5151

Driving Standards Agency
Stanley House, Talbot Street,
Nottingham NG1 5GU
0115 9557600

Electrical Contractors'
Association (ECA)
34 Palace Court, Bayswater,
London W2 4HY
0171-229 1266

Electrical Contractors' Association
of Scotland
Bush House, Bush Estate,
Midlothian EH26 0SB
0131-445 5577

Institute of Advanced
Motorists (IAM)
359 Chiswick High Road,
London W4 4HS
0181-994 4403

Institution of Electrical
Engineers (IEE)
Savoy Place,
London WC2R 0BL
0171-240 1871

Insurance Brokers Registration
Council (IBRC)
15 St Helen's Place,
London EC3A 6DS
0171-588 4387

Master Locksmiths Association
Units 4-5, The Business Park,
Woodford Halse,
Daventry NN11 3PZ
01327 262255

National Approval Council for
Security Systems (NACOSS)
Queensgate House,
14 Cookham Road,
Maidenhead SL6 8AJ
01628 37512

National Caravan Council
Catherine House, Victoria Road,
Aldershot GU11 1SS
01252 318251

National Inspection Council for
Electrical Installation Contracting
(NICEIC)
Vintage House,
37 Albert Embankment,
London SE1 7UJ
0171-582 7746

People's Dispensary for Sick
Animals (PDSA)
Whitechapel Way, Priorslee,
Telford TF2 9PQ
01952 290999

RICA
2 Marylebone Road,
London NW1 4DF
0171-830 6000

Royal National Institute for the
Blind (RNIB)
224-228 Great Portland Street,
London W1N 6AA
0171-388 1266

Royal National Institute for Deaf
People (RNID)
105 Gower Street,
London WC1E 6AH
0171-387 8033

Royal Society for the Prevention
of Accidents (RoSPA)
Cannon House,
The Priory Queensway,
Birmingham B4 6BS
0121-200 2461

Royal Society for Prevention of
Cruelty to Animals (RSPCA)
(see your local Yellow Pages)

St Andrew's Ambulance
Association
St Andrew's House,
48 Milton Street,
Glasgow G4 0HR
0141-332 4031

St John Ambulance
1 Grosvenor Crescent,
London SW1
0171-235 5231

Security Systems and Alarms
Inspection Board (SSAIB)
70/71 Camden Street,
North Shields NE30 1NH
0191-296 3242

Sold Secure PACT
Block 36,
Northumbria Police Force HQ,
Ponteland,
Newcastle upon Tyne NE20 0BL
01661 868446

Telephone Preference Service
(call the number given on your
phone bill)

INDEX